# STARCHITECTS

VISIONARY ARCHITECTS OF THE TWENTY-FIRST CENTURY

# STARCHITECTS

## VISIONARY ARCHITECTS OF THE TWENTY-FIRST CENTURY

Julio Fajardo

COLLINS DESIGN
*An Imprint of* HarperCollins*Publishers*

HarperCollins books may be purchased for educational, business, or sales promotional use.
For information, please write: Special Markets Department, HarperCollins*Publishers*,
10 East 53rd Street, New York, NY 10022.

First published in 2010 by:
Collins Design
An Imprint of HarperCollins*Publishers*
10 East 53rd Street
New York, NY 10022
Tel.: (212) 207-7000
Fax: (212) 207-7654
collinsdesign@harpercollins.com
www.harpercollins.com

Distributed throughout the world by:
HarperCollins*Publishers*
10 East 53rd Street
New York, NY 10022
Fax: (212) 207-7654

Editorial Coordinator:
Simone K. Schleifer

Assistant to Editorial Coordinator:
Aitana Lleonart

Editor and texts:
Julio Fajardo

Art Director:
Mireia Casanovas Soley

Design and layout coordination:
Claudia Martínez Alonso

Layout:
Yolanda G. Román

ISBN: 978-0-06-196877-8
Library of Congress Control Number: 2009941393

Printed in Spain
First Printing, 2010

## Contents

# Introduction

Throughout history, humans have turned to the constellations for celestial guidance, creating a relationship with the stars based on our own esoteric and metaphysical beliefs. Every culture from around the world has formed different groupings over the same planisphere, although many of these astral groups, such as Scorpio, tend to appear in most configurations. These groupings, or constellations, represent elements of daily life or accounts of feats performed by the gods. This is why we call those figures we dream of emulating or equaling *stars*: their actions, personalities, and lives loom that much larger than our own.

In 1928, the International Astronomical Union formally accepted the division of the sky into 88 constellations. Until that time, many other minor constellations had been classified, although these would later fall into disuse and today they are no longer remembered. The astronomer Eugène Delporte was entrusted with the task of establishing the definitive plan of these constellations, published by the IAU in 1930. Of the 88 constellations proposed by the IAU, the most familiar are the 12 belonging to the Zodiac—the band of sky through which the sun and planets travel. These correspond to the 12 signs astrology attributes to the horoscope and to the different characters of individuals. Also included are the 36 figures described by Ptolemy in the second century, while the 40 remaining constellations are those that have been discovered in the course of the extensive period of time we call the Modern Age.

*Starchitects: Visionary Architects of the Twenty-First Century* offers a selection—probably transitory and subjective, as all interpretations of the celestial vault have been to date—of the world's most interesting architects currently putting their name to projects, in order, among other things, to leave evidence of the progress made by our civilization on Earth. Simply stated, these *starchitects* deserve to figure in a celestial planisphere that brings together the most striking works currently being created in the field of architecture.

Among them are well-known names, the principle designers that make up the architectural Zodiac, as it were—among them, Norman Foster, Jean Nouvel and Eduardo Souto de Moura, for example—together with established firms that have been delivering projects for many years and which can be found among the most outstanding examples of world architecture. We can consider these to be "Ptolemaic architects." Additionally, there are the "rising stars," those names which, while not yet attaining international fame, probably will do so in the coming years, with work of undeniable quality.

With the intention of tracing a celestial planisphere characterizing the present state of the discipline, each architect or architectural firm is assigned a constellation designated by the IAU. Beyond a brief biography and portrait of the architect or key members of the architectural firm, each entry or "constellation" offers a sample of the architects' projects—between two and six—that situate individual work within the larger planisphere of architecture itself.

Other cultures will come and they will change the way of looking at the stars, but for us, today, these are the architects whose work makes up the main constellations in the sphere of architecture. They are the masters of design. We look to them for guidance and inspiration. They are the stars of architecture.

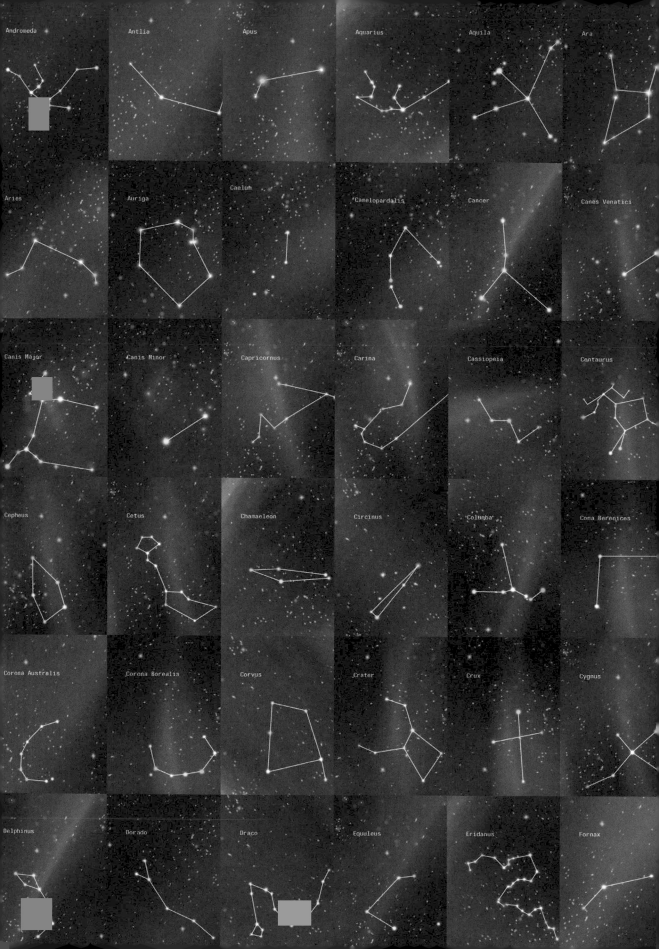

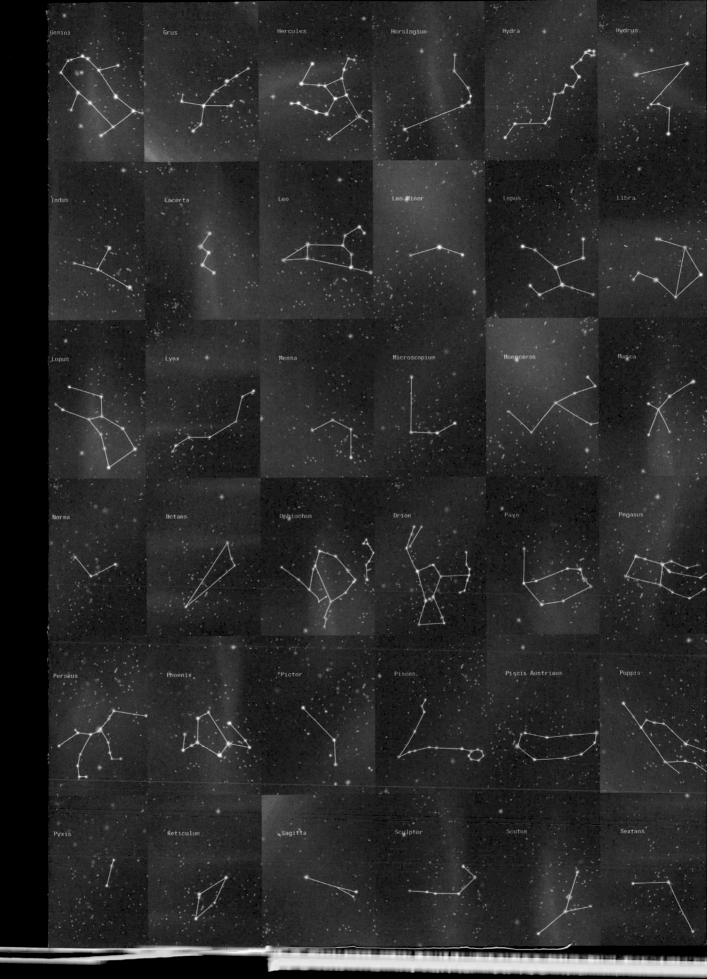

Aquila

## UNStudio

© Peter Guenzel

UNStudio
Stadhouderskade, 113
PO Box 75381
1070 AJ Amsterdam, The Netherlands
Tel.: +31 20 570 20 40
www.unstudio.com

UNStudio was founded in 1988 by Caroline Bos and Ben van Berkel. Among their goals is that of combining attention to the environment with the commitment to fulfilling their clients' wishes. Modern and stylized, their work shows deep respect for discipline. They have received major recognition for their work, including two nominations for the Mies van der Rohe Award, the 2007 Deutsche Architekturpreis for the Mercedes-Benz Museum, and the Gyproc Trophy for the Agora Theater, also in 2007.

## Mercedes-Benz Museum
Stuttgart, Germany / 2006 / Photos: © Christian Richters

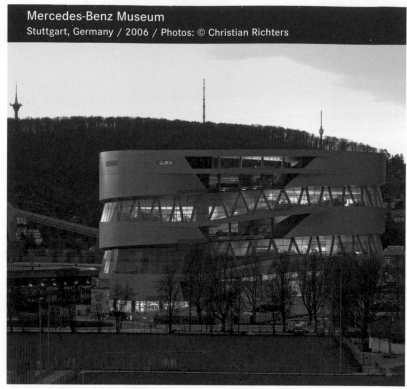

With this project, the architects faced the challenge of designing the best space possible to exhibit the history of the brand. They also questioned the very foundations of museum architecture. They created a free-form space with flowing transit ways so that visitors would truly feel surrounded by the exhibits.

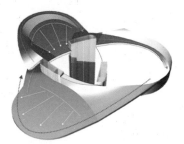

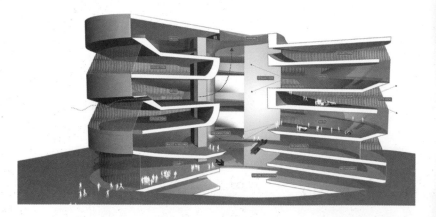

The project combines a series of spatial principles, such as the replacement of cube shapes with oblique structures and the incorporation of folds in the volumes.

The exterior of this office complex is perfectly integrated into the surrounding urban plan and features almost seamless glass façades. In the inner courtyard Its multi-colored finish gleams in different hues depending on the time of day and the incidence of sunlight to give the complex a markedly distinct character.

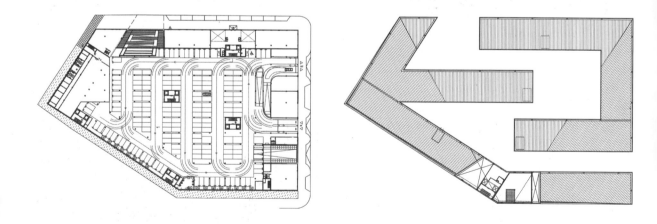

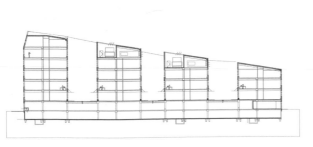

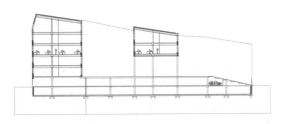

With over 23,000 m² (247,500 sq ft) of office space and 15,000 m² (161,500 sq ft) of parking, the complex has a public face—the outer façade—and a large courtyard, which is a more private space.

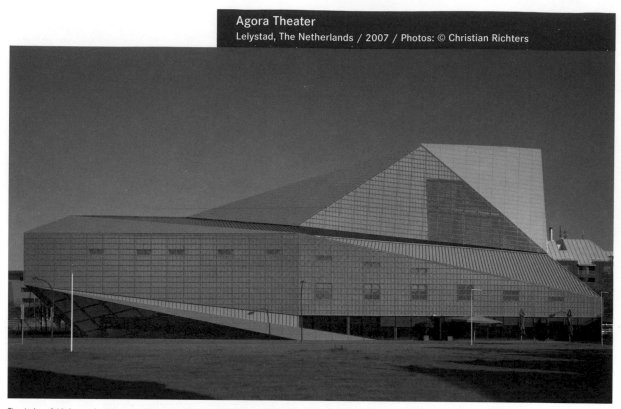

The design of this impressive theater explores the possibilities of turning the structure of these types of buildings into a work with a grand sculptural presence. A series of faceted planes and different perforations on the external layer of the façade creates a visually-arresting kaleidoscopic effect.

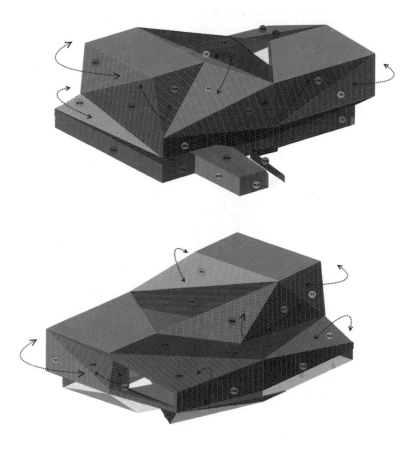

The interiors feature a large foyer with a void and a dramatic color scheme for walls with bright hues.

Set on a steeply sloping site, this single-family home takes advantage of the dramatic variation in the terrain. The box-like volume is broken into two structures—one following the incline of the site, and the other raised above the hillside.

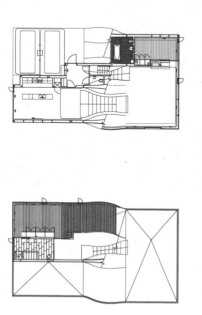

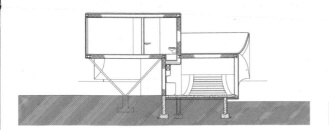

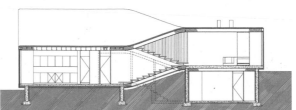

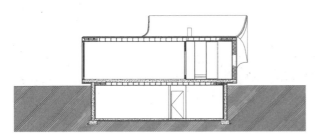

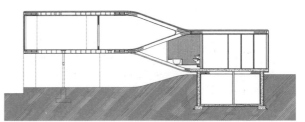

Floor-to-ceiling windows run the length of the front and rear façades. Floors and ceilings merge seamlessly in spectacular, cornerless interiors.

## Star Place Kaohsiung
Kaohsiung, Taiwan / 2008 / Photos: © Christian Richters

The creative design of this modern shopping complex is reflected in its façade. Transparent and open, it features a series of glass and aluminum panels that give a rippled effect reminiscent of spirals. An LED lighting system illuminates the façade at night with different patterns.

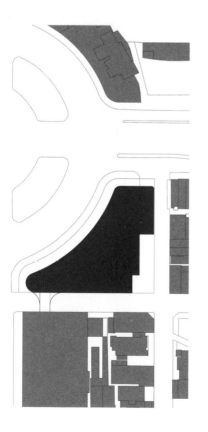

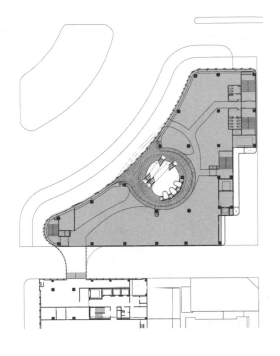

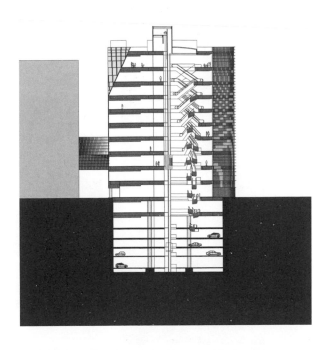

The interiors feature the same continuous spiral theme in the design of the stairs and the balconies overlooking the central atrium.

Capricornus

## Silja Tillner & Alfred Willinger

© Architekten Tillner & Willinger

Architekten Tillner & Willinger
Margaretenplatz, 7/2/1
1050 Vienna, Austria
Tel.: +43 1 3106859
www.tw-arch.at

Founded by Silja Tillner in 1995, this architecture practice was joined by partner Alfred Willinger in 2003, with the name changed to its present one in 2007. With particular focus on public building and urban design work, their projects feature the construction of modern membrane structures, intelligent buildings geared toward sustainability, and office spaces, among others. They received the 2000 Bauhaus Award for the Urbion project in Vienna, and the 2005 Leaf Award for the best regeneration project.

## Skyline Spittelau
Vienna, Austria / 2008 / Photos: © Werner Kaligofsky

This building is one of the key projects of the Gürtel ring road transformation. The former railroad route now encompasses the complex, while the arches of the raised street car system serve as a plinth for the building.

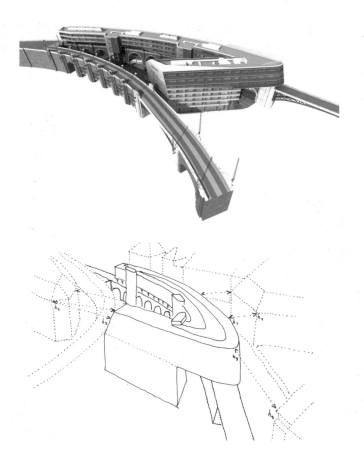

The double façade is conical in shape on the side overlooking Heiligenstädter Strasse.

## Urban Loritz Platz
Vienna, Austria / 2000 / Photos: © Monika Nikolic

Designed to provide a sheltered area for an important transport hub in the Austrian capital, this square is crossed by street car lines, cycle tracks, and crosswalks, encouraging use of this light and airy structure.

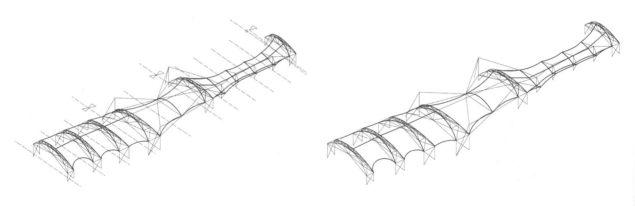

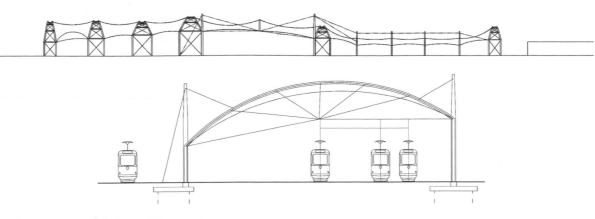

The translucent membrane covering the site becomes a screen when the lighting system comes on at night.

The remodeling project for this historic building in the center of Vienna features the choice of an elegant, sparsely decorated glass main façade. The sides and rear feature a grid of perforated aluminum louvers.

The highest floors house luxury apartments, while the lower levels are given over to European Union-related activities.

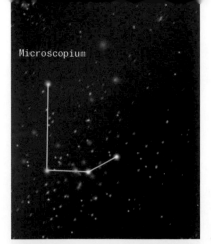

Microscopium

## Matija Bevk & Vasa J. Perović

© Vasa J. Perović, Matija Bevk

**Bevk Perović Arhitekti**
**Tobačna, 5**
**1000 Ljubljana, Slovenia**
**Tel.: +38 61 241 76 30**
**www.bevkperovic.com**

Vasa J. Perović was born in 1965 in Belgrade, Yugoslavia. In 1992 he graduated from the Faculty of Architecture of the city's university and obtained a master's degree in architecture between 1992 and 1994. In 1997 he founded the firm that is now known as Bevk Perović Arhitekti. Born in 1972 in Slovenia, Matija Bevk graduated from the University of Ljubljana in 1999. Together they have received acknowledgments such as the 2007 Emerging Architect Special Mention in the European Union Contemporary Architecture Awards and the Mies van der Rohe Award for the University of Ljubljana Faculty of Mathematics in the same year.

## Brdo Congress Centre
Kranj, Slovenia / 2009 / Photos: © Miran Kambič

Built for the Slovenian presidency of the European Union, this complex lies in a setting shared with a medieval castle. The volume is a low glass pavilion contained in the outline of an old castle outbuilding.

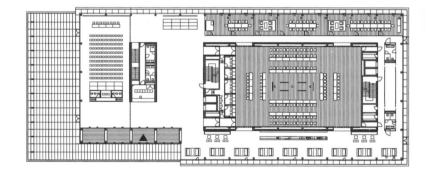

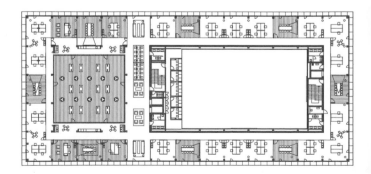

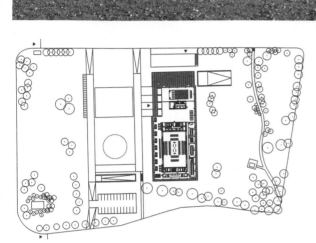

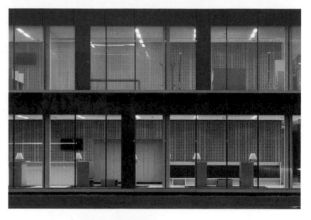

The lower level houses public halls while the upper level contains offices.

An abandoned quarry is the unusual setting for this modern residential complex. The 140 apartments are laid out in a complex of two buildings divided by bands that outline the passageways.

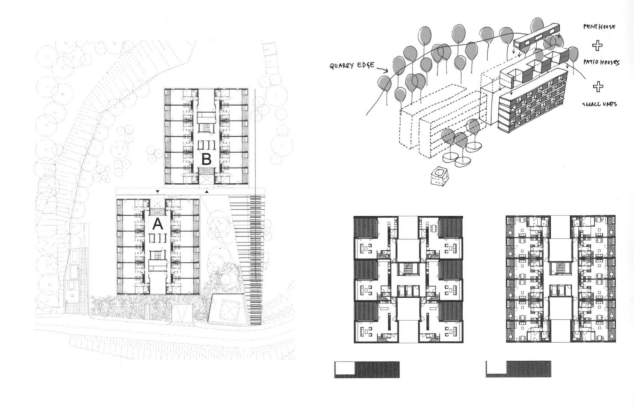

The façade creates patterns with dark glass and balconies lined with yellow panels.

## House D
Ljubljana, Slovenia / 2007 / Photos: © Miran Kambič

Located in a residential neighborhood of luxury single-family houses, this dwelling greatly responds to the requirements of the owners, who wanted a home with a living room, one bedroom and a gymnasium.

Each of the levels establishes a different degree of privacy and relation with the exterior.

## House K
### Domžale, Slovenia / 2008 / Photos: © Miran Kambič

A strictly horizontal layout is the striking feature of this simple single-family residence. The elongated shape of the volume was designed for a glass wall linking the interior with the landscaped area.

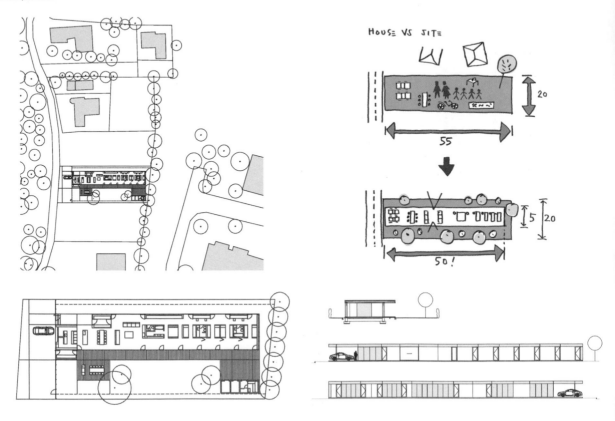

A long passageway runs the length of the floor and connects the different spaces, which are actually a single room.

This building is located on the banks of a river in the Slovenian capital and contains 56 rooms for university students. The program for this project was clear—multiple uses. The building is used for teaching, community living, and leisure activities.

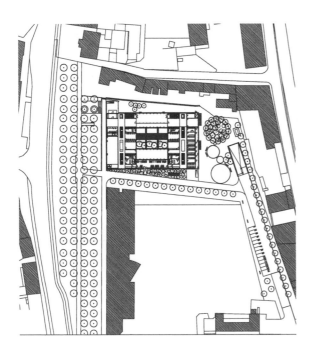

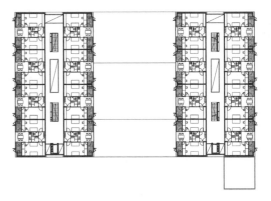

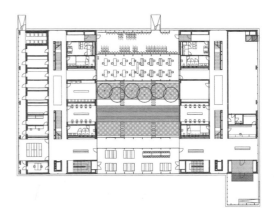

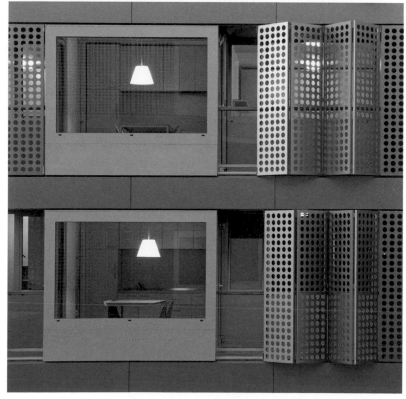

The rooms are laid out around common areas where the bathrooms, kitchens and dining rooms are located.

Lepus

Emil Urbel

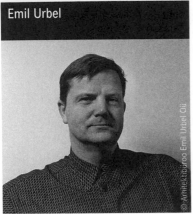

**Arhitektibüroo Emil Urbel Oü**
**Kentmanni, 15-1**
**10116 Tallinn, Estonia**
**Tel.: +372 661 6250**
**www.emilurbel.ee**

Emil Urbel was born in Pämu, Estonia, in 1959 and graduated from the Estonian Academy of Arts in 1982. He has been a member of the Union of Estonian Architects since then, and in the period from 1995 through 2000 he taught at the school he graduated from in the 1980s. He also taught at the University of Applied Sciences in Tallinn until 2005. In 1990 he was given the European Union prize for best young architect. He was a partner of Architects Urbel ja Pei Oü from 1989 until 2000, when he founded his own practice.

## Aaviku Residences
Tallinn, Estonia / 2003 / Photos: © Kalle Veesaar

This low-cost housing development features four types of homes, depending on the number of occupants. The owner of each lot was able to choose the layout of the home and the color of the façade, provided two adjoining houses were not of the same color.

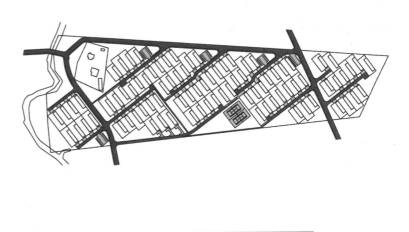

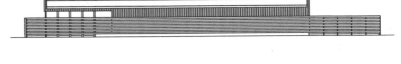

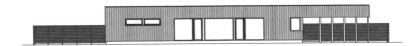

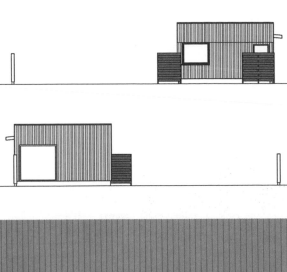

The simple habitats are built from prefabricated wooden panels.

The large front window dominating the main façade is not the only source of natural light for this two-level residence. A series of skylights in the roof also provides the interior with light.

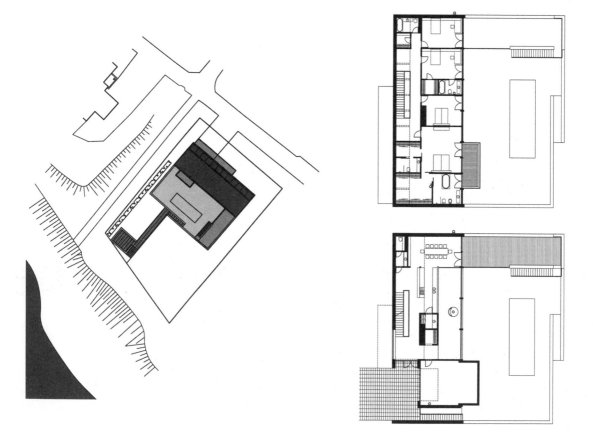

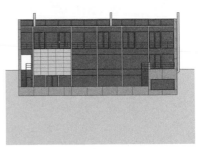

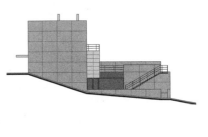

The sea views were largely the determining factor for the form and orientation of the house.

The living area receives the most light, and is the space around which the different rooms and transit areas of this single-family residence are laid out. Its great height made possible the installation of large windows in the upper part.

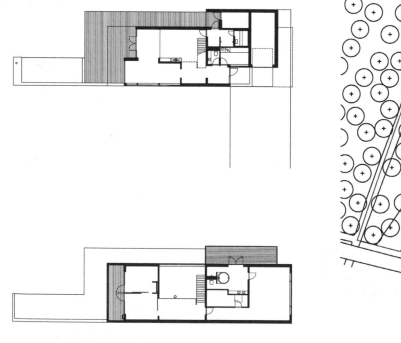

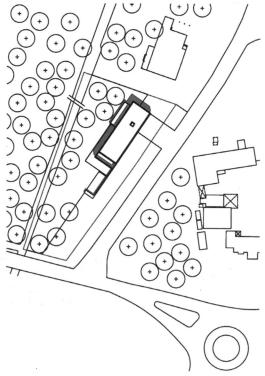

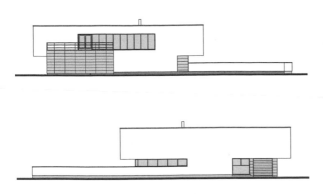

The flue leading from the fireplace becomes a striking decorative element and provides visual continuity to the lower and upper levels.

Crater

Julien de Smedt

© Claus Larsen

JDS Architects
Vesterbrogade, 69 D
1620 Copenhagen V, Denmark
Tel.: +45 3378 1010
www.jdsarchitects.com

With offices in the Danish capital, in Oslo, and in Brussels, Julien de Smedt's practice is one of the highest profile young architectural firms in Europe. A former collaborator at Rem Kool-haas's OMA, Julien de Smedt was a guest professor at Rice University in Houston, and has worked as a lecturer at the University of Kentucky. His design work has received recognition such as the Golden Lion at the Venice Biennale, the Henning Larsen Award in 2003, and an Eckersberg Medal in 2005.

# Holmenkollen Ski Jump
## Oslo, Norway / 2010 / Renderings: © JDS Architects

This project is sure to play a major role in this ski resort close to Oslo. The slender lines of the structure have been accentuated, so that it seems to be held up by the art of magic and connect directly with the sky.

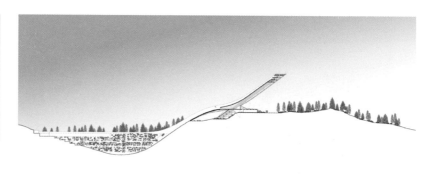

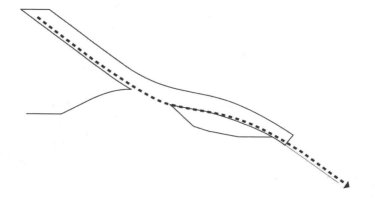

The external face of the volume is designed as a single uninterrupted strip, mimicking the actual ramp.

This building is the second stage of a residential project previously commissioned by the same client, although on this occasion two thirds of the space was for parking and one third for homes.

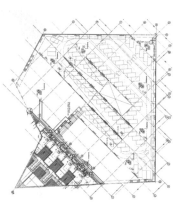
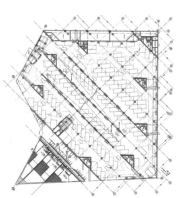
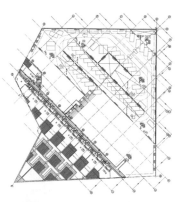

The stepped typology enabled gardens to be built on roofs, and offered panoramic views from balconies.

## Docklands Residential Complex
Aarhus, Denmark / 2010 / Renderings © JDS Architects

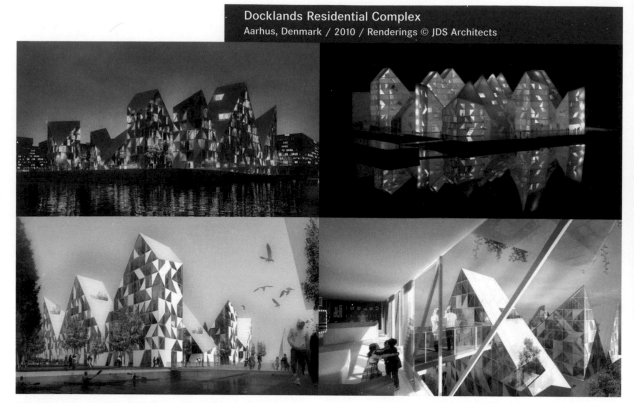

This project provides an opportunity for a former cargo terminal in Denmark's second largest city to be developed as a residential complex. The project is designed as a series of icebergs and will contain 200 apartments.

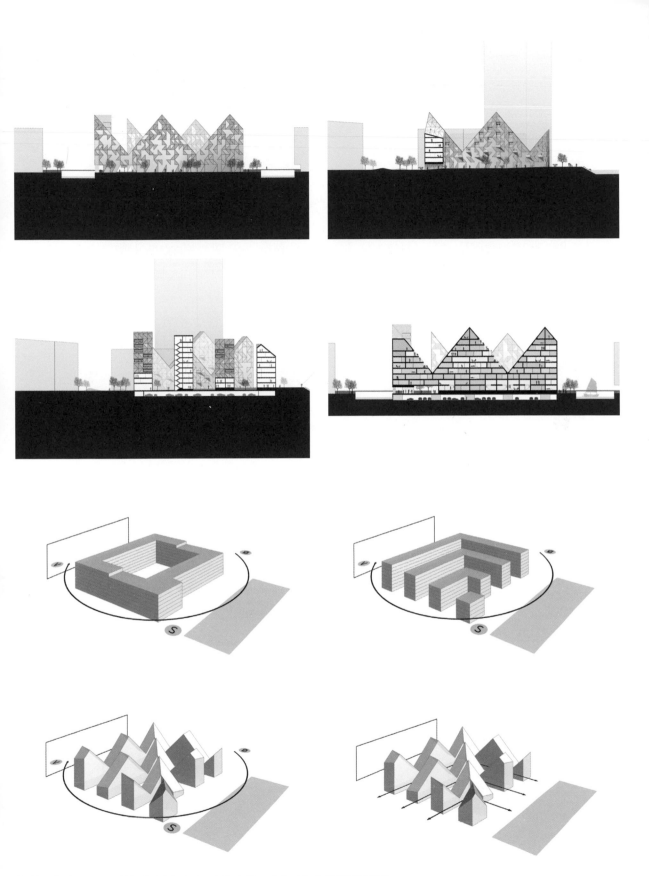

The triangular shapes are overlaid as fractals to give form to the buildings, in the style of a Sierpinski pyramid.

The client's brief for this high-rise building was the following: it had to be 666 or 888 m (2,185 or 2,913 ft) tall—in the end it will reach 1,111 m (3,645 ft)—and have a surface area of 5 million m² (53,819,500 sq ft). The project also had to follow strict feng shui principles in its essence.

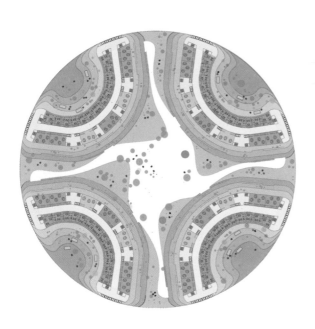

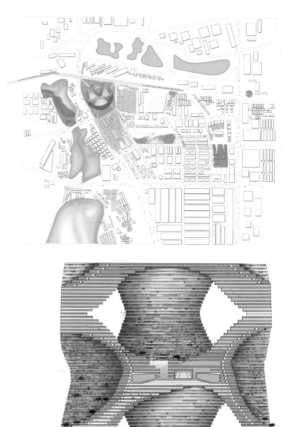

The project is part of a major urban renewal experienced by the city of Shenzhen, finally connected to Hong Kong by a bridge.

Sinuous arabesques observed on a beach or in a mosaic seem to have been the source of inspiration for the design of this retail complex with volumes that are submerged almost unnoticeably and emerge again to configure basements and galleries with highly organic forms.

The upper level is covered by a green space that turns the complex into a park and adapts it masterfully to its coastal setting.

Cygnus

## Moshe Safdie

© Stephen Kelly

Moshe Safdie & Associates
100 Properzi Way
Sommerville, MA 02143, USA
Tel.: +1 617 629 2100
www.msafdie.com

Born in Israel in 1938, Moshe Safdie spent his youth in Canada, where he graduated from McGill University in 1961. After collaborating with Louis I. Kahn, he returned to Montreal where his architectural practice was located until 1978, the year he moved his office to Boston, after having taught at Yale. As of that time, the architect embarked on major projects such as the Museum of Civilization in Quebec and the National Gallery of Canada. Among his most outstanding acknowledgments are the Royal Architectural Institute of Canada's Prix du XX$^e$ Siècle and the AIA Award for Excellence.

## Khalsa Memorial Complex
Anandpur Sahib, India / 2009 / Photos: © Michal Ronnen Safdie

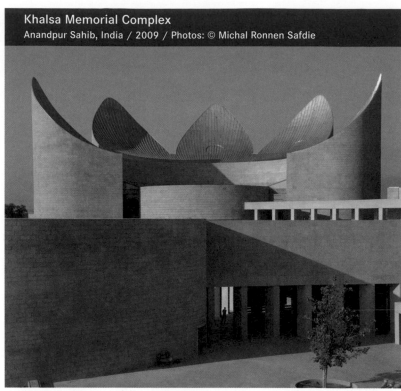

This new museum dedicated to Sikh culture is located in the holy city of Anandpur Sahib. The volume is laid out around a great plaza and contains a 400-seat auditorium, a two-story library, and several exhibition rooms.

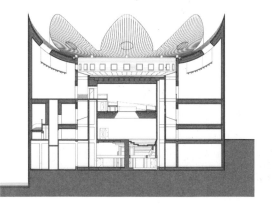

The roof folds give the complex monumental character.

This triangular public building provides space for five levels of library, in addition to an imposing crescent-shaped retainer wall, which makes it an architectural landmark for the surrounding area.

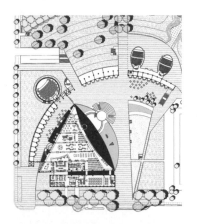

Inside, transit areas are bathed in light entering through the endless windows.

This mixed-use complex is arranged around a central axis that extends from the sea to Singapore's urban grid. Its design features three 50-story towers and more than 2,600 hotel rooms.

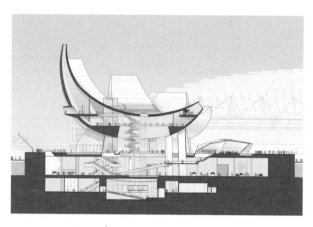

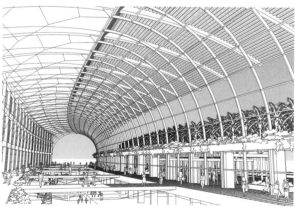

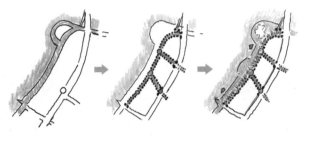

The complex will also house a casino and two 2,000-seat theaters.

The rebuilding of the Yad Vashem Museum included a new reception building plus another building for exhibitions, different pavilions, a synagogue, and a series of educational and video facilities.

Yad vashem. Thoughts on a scheme.

Most of this Holocaust museum is underground, with only the conical structure of the Hall of Names rising above the surface.

Andromeda

Steven Holl

© Mark Heitoff

Steven Holl Architects
450 West 31st Street, 11th floor
New York, NY 10001, USA
Tel.: +1 212 629 7262
www.stevenholl.com

Steven Holl was born in Bremerton, Washington in 1947. He graduated from the University of Washington and continued his studies in Rome. In 1976 he founded Steven Holl Architects in New York. Considered one of the best architects in the United States, Holl has been praised for his skill in mixing space and light while showing great interest in context. Among other awards, he has won the AIA 2007 Institute Honor Award and the National Design Award in Architecture. He teaches at the Columbia University School of Architecture.

## Nelson-Atkins Museum of Art
Kansas City, MO, USA / 2007 / Photos: © Andy Ryan

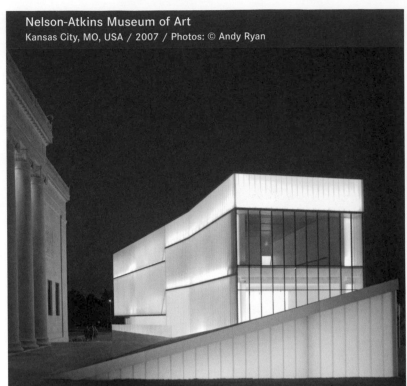

The Bloch Building is a new structure erected next to the museum's main building. Located in a sculpture garden, the new addition is like another piece of the collection. The architect's intention was for visitors to experience the interweaving of light, art, architecture, and landscape.

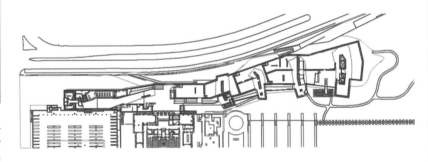

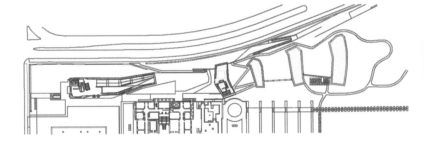

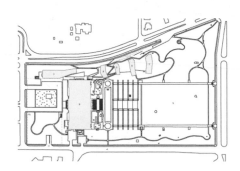

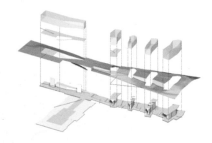

The glass foyer is illuminated at night as a draw for the public to attend the different exhibitions held by the museum.

The architect connects two of the school's buildings with this structure. The striking transparency of the façade provides the complex with a space full of light which becomes the predominant focal point. These four stories greatly revitalize the center.

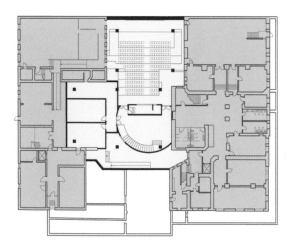

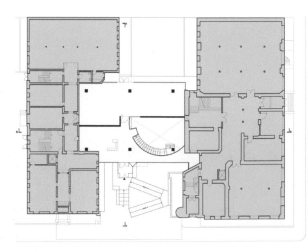

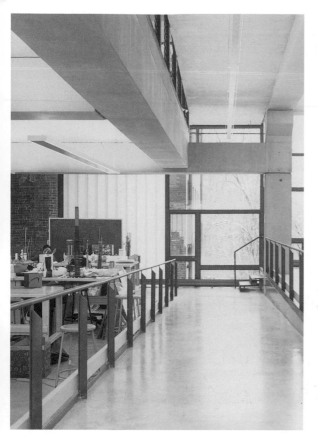

Standing out among the new spaces is the auditorium, located in the basement with seating arranged on a slight incline.

This undergraduate residence was designed to convey the idea of porosity. Its 10 stories are hidden behind a cement grid and shine outwardly through the small squares of the façade to create a striking magic lantern effect.

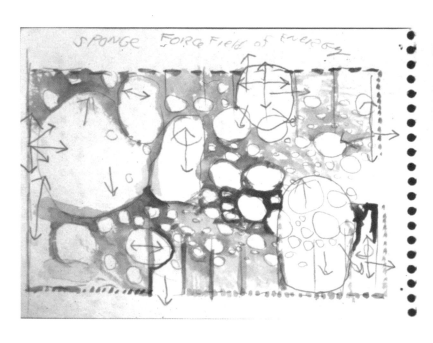

The combination of the façade's translucent effect with the different colors of the cladding is spectacular.

## Linked Hybrid
Beijing, China / 2009 / Photos: © Iwan Baan

This development of over 220,000 m² (2,340,000 sq ft) offers a modern and pedestrian-centered urban space. Connected by a network of passageways, Linked Hybrid is a "city within a city" combining residential, commercial, educational, and leisure land uses.

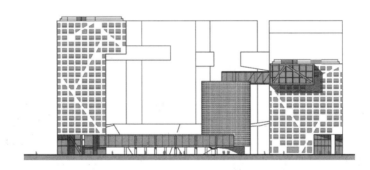

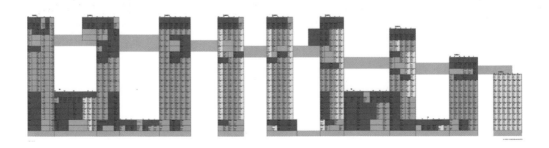

Between the 12th and 18th floors there are spaces housing a swimming pool, fitness room, café, and an art gallery.

Carina

## Jean Marc Ibos & Myrto Vitart

© R. Schroeder

Jean Marc Ibos & Myrto Vitart
4, Cité Paradis
75010 Paris, France
Tel.: +33 1 44 83 85 80
www.ibosvitart.com

Jean Marc Ibos & Myrto Vitart established their practice in 1990. During the first half of the decade both were guest professors at the École Spéciale d'Architecture in Paris. They would repeat the experience in 2005–2006 at the École Polytechnique Fédérale in Lausanne, Switzerland. Among their acknowledgments are the 2008 Brittany Architecture Prize, being named Knights of the National Order of Merit (France) in 2002, and the 1998 DuPont Benedictus Award for the Lille Museum of Fine Arts. Outstanding among their works are the Lille Museum of Fine Arts, the Nanterre Fire Station and the André Malraux Library.

## André Malraux Library
Strasbourg, France / 2008 / Photos: © Georges Fessy, Philippe Ruault

After a spectacular transformation, the old Seegmuller warehouses were turned into a modern médiathèque (media library) by means of a project that gave particular focus to the design of its interiors and corporate identity.

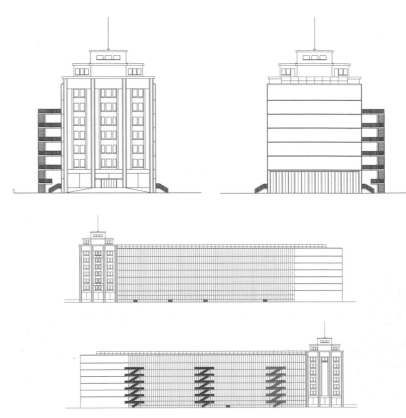

The spectacular effect of red vinyl gives visual impact to interior spaces.

To deign this new hospital department, Jean Marc Ibos and Myrto Vitart focused on the creation of a space that would welcome visitors, a place where the exterior would blend almost seamlessly with internal areas. This was achieved through the size and spaciousness of the foyer.

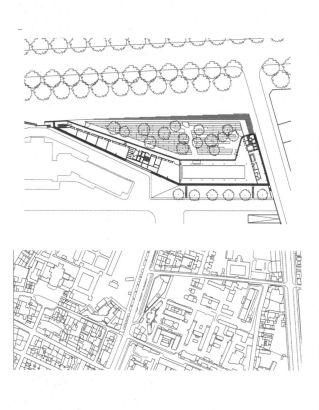

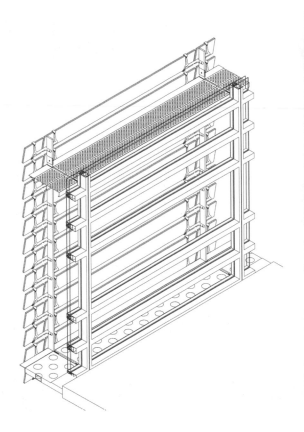

The project was able to create relaxing spaces that feature views of the outside.

The challenge of designing a fire station lies in guaranteeing access to vehicles from any point of the building in as short a time as possible. A horizontal, open-plan layout was chosen for this, with volumes arranged around a central service courtyard.

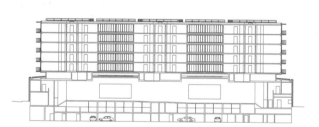

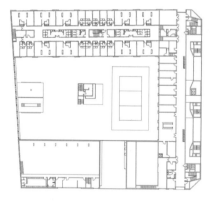

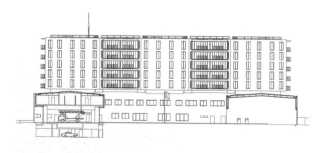

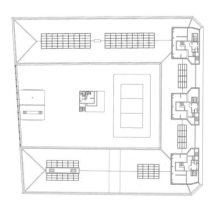

A spirit of modern austerity is behind the design of the station interiors.

Influencing the layout of this building is the archives unit, comprising independent cells. Although compressed, it is the equivalent of 18 km (11 miles) of shelves. The space unfolds horizontally to create a succession of masses and voids interconnected with the areas of public access.

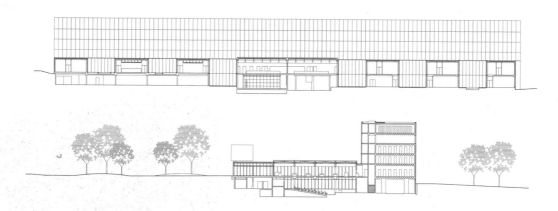

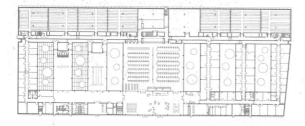

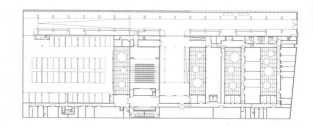

The exhibition area, auditorium and reading room are laid out around courtyards.

Lynx

Nuno
& José Mateus

José Mateus

Nuno Mateus

ARX Portugal Arquitectos lda.
Largo de Santos, 4, 1º
1200-808 Lisbon, Portugal
Tel.: +351 213 918 110
www.arx.pt

Nuno Mateus was born in Castelo Branco in 1961 and completed his studies at the Faculty of Architecture of the Technical University of Lisbon in 1984. He then went on to graduate with a master's degree from Columbia University in 1987. His brother José was born two years later and also studied at the same university. In 1991 they established the ARX practice. Together they have received the Chicago Athenaeum International Architecture Award and the International Association of Art Critics Award, in addition to a nomination for the Mies van der Rohe Award in 2002 for the Ílhavo Maritime Museum.

## Barreiro College of Technology
Barreiro, Portugal / 2007 / Photos: © FG & SG

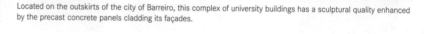

Located on the outskirts of the city of Barreiro, this complex of university buildings has a sculptural quality enhanced by the precast concrete panels cladding its façades.

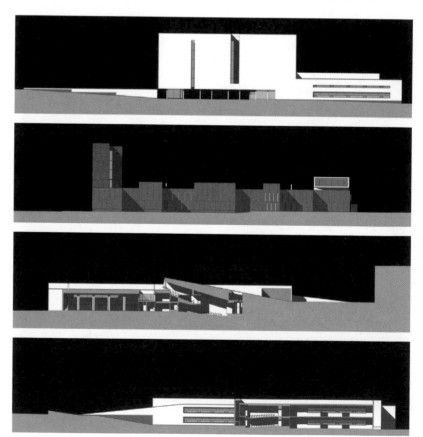

The bareness of the green areas surrounding the complex provides an aspect of modernity and space that does not make the buildings any less imposing.

This flat-roofed white house evokes a series of basic characteristics of traditional Portuguese architecture, although modernized with cantilevered rooflines and partially open courtyards.

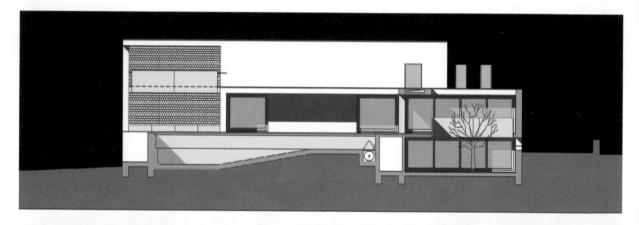

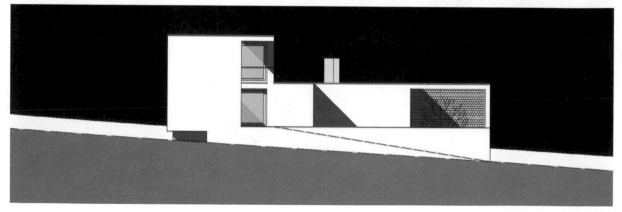

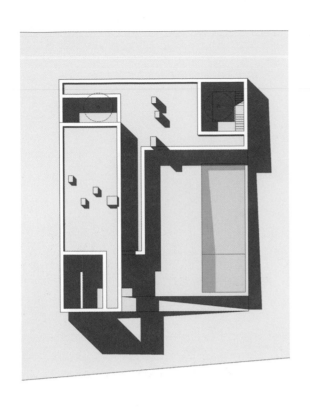

A series of skylights and clerestory windows guarantees plentiful sunlight entering interior spaces.

Located in the country and bounded by stone walls with a strong rural character, the site of this residence is a south-facing hillside. A long volume was designed for this terrain, opening to the outside through a large glass façade.

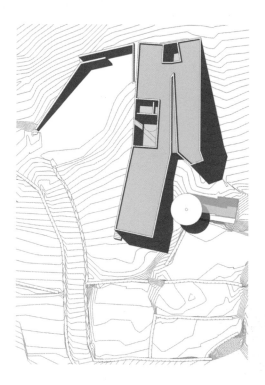

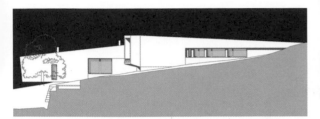

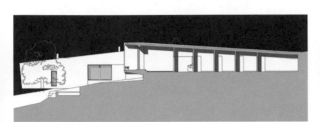

A narrow passageway connects the northern side, overlooking a courtyard, with the southern side, which is completely open to the landscape.

Built over the ruins of an 18th-century house of which only the remains of the façade and chapel were standing, this library is located in a part of the town that was somewhat fragmented in nature, and which this project has served to consolidate.

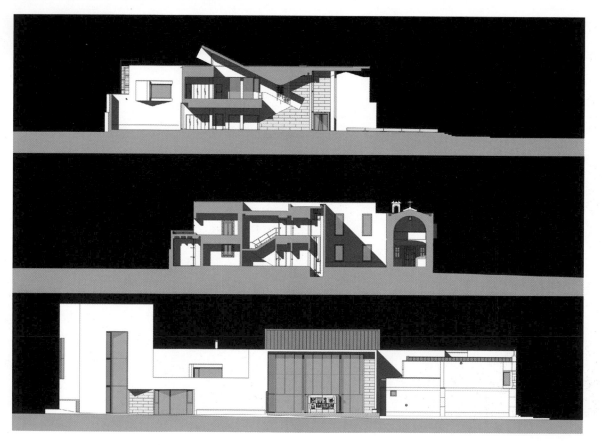

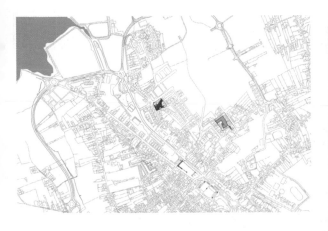

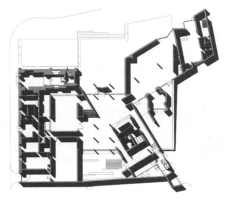

The chapel was restored for religious use, but with a much more contemporary style.

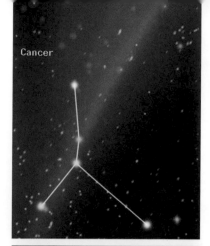
Cancer

## Bregman & Hamann Architects

Douglas Birkenshaw
Karen Cvornyek
David Stavros
Paul Gogan

Bregman & Hamann Architects
481 University Avenue, suite 300
Toronto M5G 2H4, Ontario, Canada
Tel.: +1 416 596 2299
www.bharchitects.com

Established in Toronto in 1953, Bregman & Hamann Architects is one of the most prestigious practices in Canada. With offices in Vancouver, Shanghai, United Arab Emirates, and India, the firm has collaborated with such names as Mies van der Rohe, Santiago Calatrava, and Daniel Libeskind. During the more than 55 years of its existence, the firm has specialized in large building projects and currently has a commission to build a total of nine million m² (99 million sq ft), with a total cost of eight billion dollars.

## Hong Kong New World Tower
### Shanghai, China / 2003 / Photos: © Kerun Ip

Located in one of the most buoyant business districts in Shanghai, this 58-story building contains a five-star hotel occupying 34,000 m² (366,000 sq ft), another 25,000 m² (269,999 sq ft) of commercial space, nearly 20,000 m² (215,000 sq ft) of luxury apartments, and 15,000 m² (161,500 sq ft) of office space.

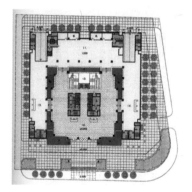

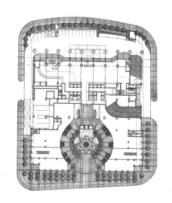

A four-story plinth leads to the more slender main volume of the building and forms a transition with the street it overlooks.

This gigantic complex houses the Sheraton Shanghai Hotel, in addition to space for offices, apartments, and retail galleries. The hotel has 525 rooms, and the total area of the complex exceeds 200,000 m² (2,152,850 sq ft).

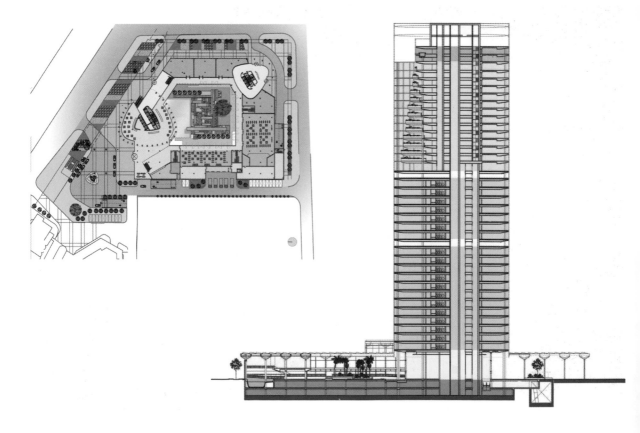

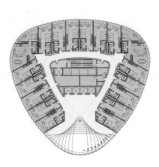

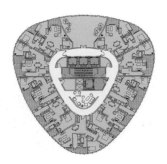

The large dimensions of the towers enable the foyers to be spacious and occupy several levels.

This residential development in the Jinan district is on a 69,000 m² (742,700 sq ft) site. Overlooking two artificial lakes, the complex features a series of 400 m² (4,305 sq ft) luxury penthouses with panoramic windows. The volumes vary in height: they are mostly in a range of 18-30 stories, but some vary between 6 and 12 stories.

The façade design takes its inspiration from water, reflected in its organic and sinuous shape.

Designed in collaboration with the Daniel Libeskind studio, the extension to the Royal Ontario Museum gives a starring role to glass. The new volumes, pointed and almost crashing into each other, are reminiscent of naturally formed crystals. These interconnected structures create a series of public spaces that make a true architectural statement.

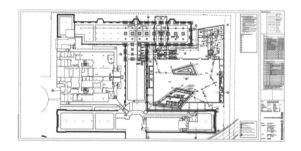

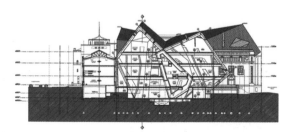

Another integral part of the project was the redesign of nine galleries to house the museum's collections.

This new university building is located between two already-existing structures. With three levels and a central atrium formed by balconies, the center provides study and research spaces with easy transit and a variety of common areas.

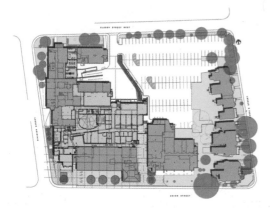

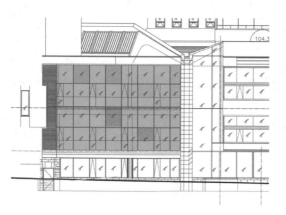

Designed in collaboration with students, the center features a wall that filters particles from the air before distributing it around the interiors.

Sextans

Joaquín Torres
& Rafael Llamazares

A-cero
Parque Empresarial La Finca
Paseo Club Deportivo, 1, bloque 6 A
28223 Pozuelo de Alarcón
Madrid, Spain
Tel.: +34 91 799 7984
www.a-cero.com

Founded in 1996, the A-cero architecture firm currently has offices in Madrid, A Coruña, and Dubai. A new office in the Dominican Republic is opening soon. Led by Joaquín Torres, the firm's philosophy is to start with a general concept with a somewhat sculptural value, before developing the architectural details of each project. Particularly renowned for their single-family homes, the practice is currently creating a client base in order to create more varied design typologies.

## Residence · 147
Madrid, Spain / 2008 / Photos: © Santiago Cobreros

The design of this single-family home features a relationship between the volumes, the use of glass walls, abrupt cantilevered structures and the large interior spaces, standard in A-cero projects.

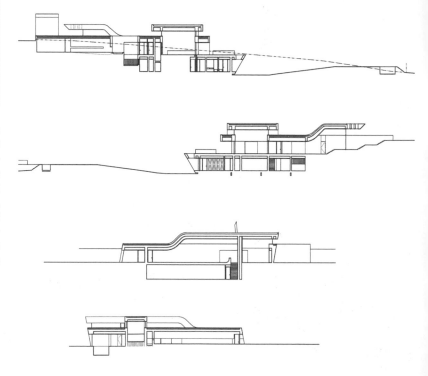

To make the best use of the sloping site, the house was designed to enable the different horizontal volumes to be stacked in layers.

This project consists of six islands in the artificial archipelago being built in Dubai. The complex will include six hotels, an aquarium, schools, daycare centers, a convention center, leisure and night life area, and a residential area.

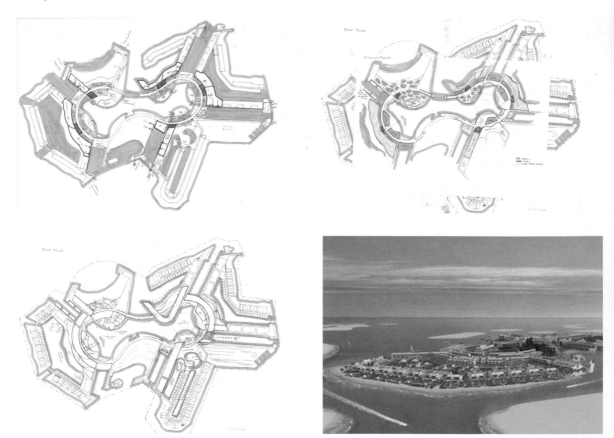

The technical challenge is huge: development has to take place in the sea, 5 km (3 miles) from the coast.

This single-family home is a clear example of the general guiding philosophy of A-cero architects. Starting with a sculptural shape, the spaces are defined to create more versatile rooms that are easy to live in.

The elegant simplicity of the façade makes use of the austerity provided by marble, a material commonly used by the firm.

Located on a plot covering 3,502 m² (37,700 sq ft), this house takes the form of a Greek cross. Functional and open to the exterior, the house has excellent views of the surrounding area. The interior is laid out by function, and the visual and spatial effect of the staircase in the foyer is striking, as is the double height overlooking the living area.

Each of the three levels of the house has a specific and independent use.

The site of this development is trapezoidal and sloping, which underlines the stepped design of the complex. Each of the houses has floor space of 450 m² (4,850 sq ft) and three stories. Entry is through the lower level, while the spacious living area and kitchen are on the intermediate level.

The bedrooms and private areas are located on the top floor of each house.

## Bernard Tschumi

**Bernard Tschumi Architects**
**227 West 17th Street, 2nd floor**
**New York, NY 10011, USA**
**Tel.: +1 212 807 6340**
**www.tschumi.com**

Bernard Tschumi Architects was initially established in Paris in 1983. However, since 1988, after receiving the commission for the Parc de la Villette, the main office has been in New York. Nicknamed "the most discreet internationally-renowned architects," Bernard Tschumi has held teaching positions at universities such as Princeton and Cooper Union. His work has been exhibited at a number of institutions including the Museum of Modern Art in New York, the Venice Biennale, and the Centre Pompidou in Paris. The awards he has received include the Grand Prix National d'Architecture and the National Endowment for the Arts.

## Blue Residential Tower
New York, NY, USA / 2007 / Photos: © Bernard Tschumi Architects

This 16-story residential tower on Manhattan's Lower East Side contains 32 apartments plus commercial space on the first and third floors. Its iconic feature is the continuous sloping wall, present in many of the apartments.

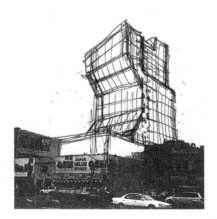

The complex enjoys wonderful views over the Williamsburg Bridge.

Located adjacent to the Makriyianni excavations, this museum was designed specifically to house the Parthenon Marbles and a series of archaeological collections dating from Ancient Greece. With visitor numbers at around 10,000 per day, it was important to make movement through the building easy.

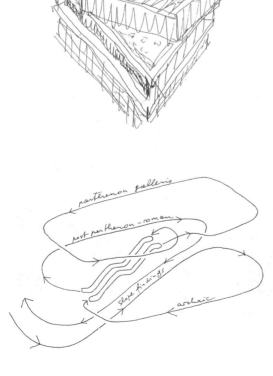

The total cost of the project was 60 million dollars (41.7 million euros).

With the aim of preserving the identity of a culturally vibrant community, this residential project has been specially designed to be built over a series of existing structures, and with a total area of 100 ha (247 ac). The project was inspired by the layout of Factory 798, an industrial complex standing on the same site in the 1950s.

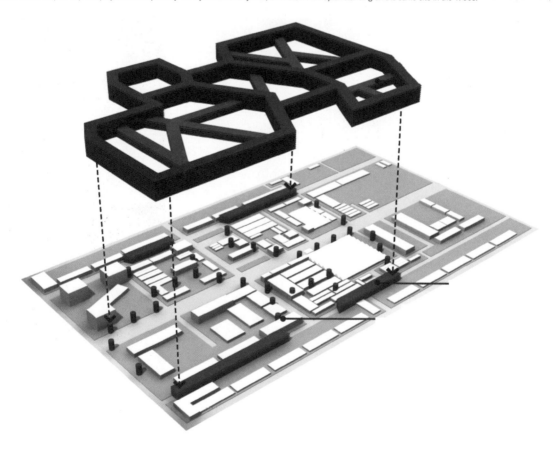

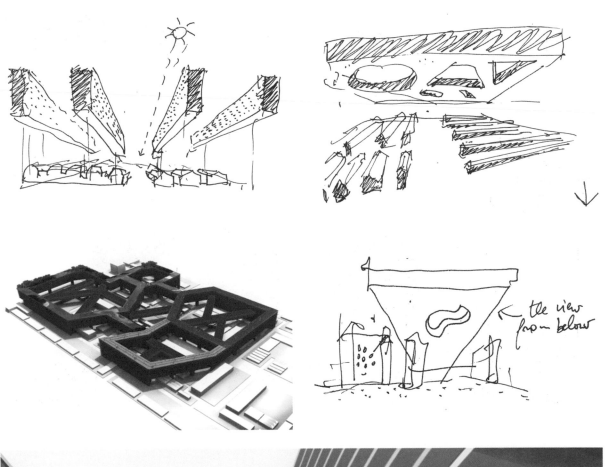

the view from below

The raised and floating structures are the most visually-striking element of the complex.

Winner of a competition held four years before construction began, this project for a school of architecture included a classroom block, a lecture hall, offices, a large courtyard, and gardens laid out over different levels.

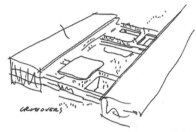

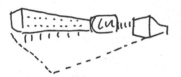

The project cost 14 million dollars (9.7 million euros) to build.

## University of Cincinnati Athletic Center
Cincinnati, OH, USA / 2006 / Photos: © Bernard Tschumi Architects

This sports complex contains spaces for offices, training rooms, classrooms, locker rooms, and an athletics track with stands holding up to 45,000 spectators.

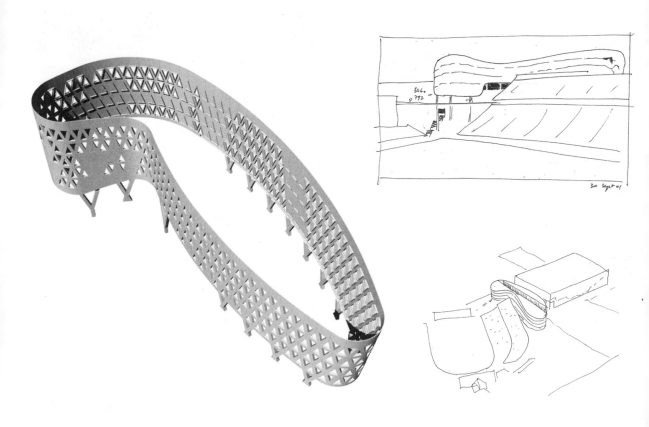

Located literally at the heart of the campus, the complex has become one of its most architecturally distinct features.

Known by the name of "elliptic city," this financial center covers an area of previously unpopulated land and extends as a series of islands in an elliptic artificial archipelago.

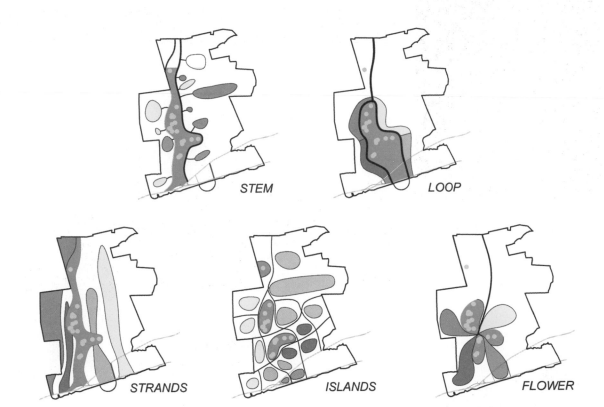

STEM

LOOP

STRANDS

ISLANDS

FLOWER

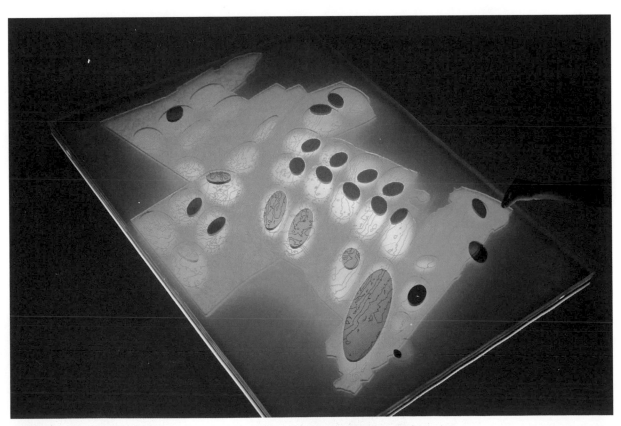

From the air, the different shapes of the buildings, surrounded by lush vegetation, resemble toy geometric blocks that fit into a base.

Centaurus

## Mario Botta

© Beat Pfändler

Mario Botta
Via Ciani, 16
6904 Lugano, Switzerland
Tel.: +41 91 972 86 25
www.botta.ch

Born in Ticino in 1943, Mario Botta studied at the University Institute of Architecture in Venice. He began his practice in Lugano in 1970. Founder of the Mendrisio Academy of Architecture, he has received acknowledgment of great significance such as the AIA Merit Award for Excellence for the San Francisco Museum of Modern Art, and the Europa Nostra Award for the remodeling of La Scala in Milan. Among his most outstanding projects are the André Malraux Cultural Center in Chambéry, the Jean Tinguely Museum in Basel, and Évry cathedral, in the town of Évry, France.

## Church of Santo Volto
Turin, Italy / 2006 / Photos: © Enrico Cano

Hollow towers rise from the structure of this church as skylights that bathe the interior with light. These volumes are held up by means of a simple pair of pillars.

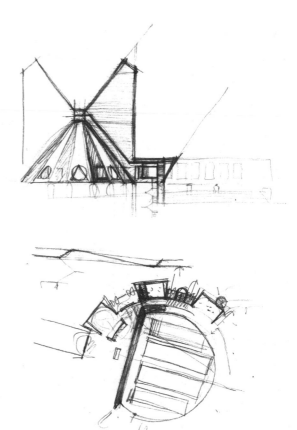

The helical form rising above the dome has become a unique feature of the project.

Set on a hillside in the Piombino countryside, this winery presents visitors with a large cylinder cut by a diagonal plane that runs parallel to the slope of the terrain. Two porticoed wings point toward the sea.

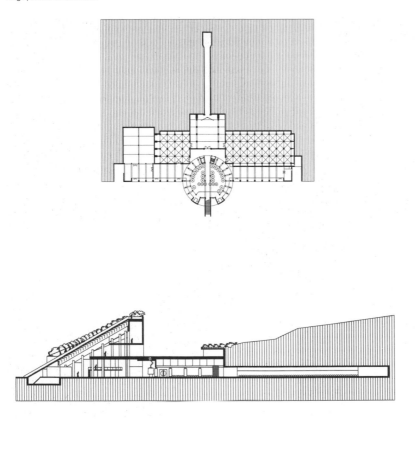

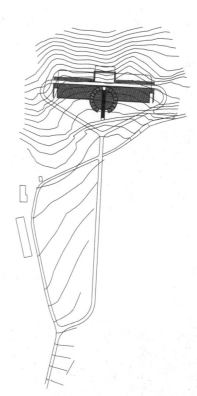

The elements required for winemaking also play a leading role in the interior architecture.

These twin 117 m (384 ft) towers stand out particularly for their unusual brick cladding, uncommon in buildings of their size. The two volumes rise from a three-story plinth with a spacious foyer.

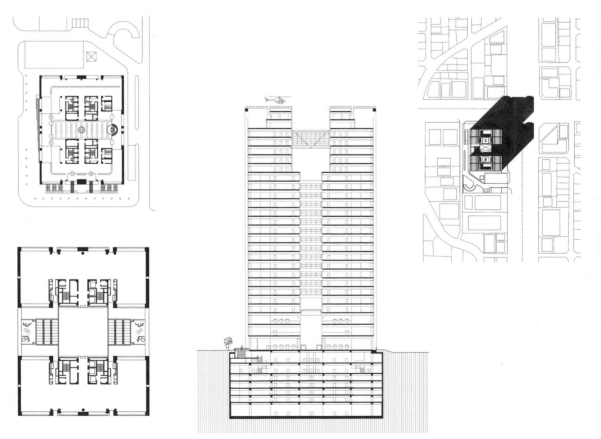

The buildings have a frame made from steel and reinforced concrete. The rectangular brick panels are prefabricated elements.

This spa and wellness center emerges discreetly as a series of projections that overlook the surrounding mountainous landscape. The interior spaces are laid out over four levels, with a large swimming pool on the third level.

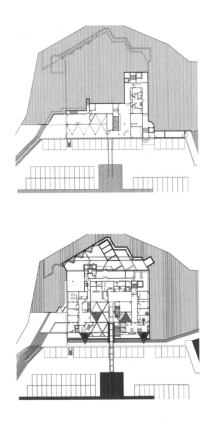

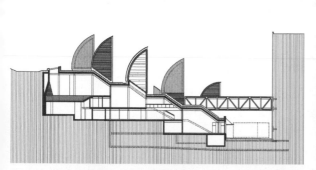

The high ceilings create a feeling of openness in spaces that are perfect for relaxation.

Reticulum

## John & Patricia Patkau

Patkau Architects
1564 West 6th Avenue
Vancouver V6J 1R2
British Columbia, Canada
Tel.: +1 604 683 7633
www.patkau.ca

With three principals—John Patkau, Patricia Patkau and Michael Cunningham—and three associates, this Vancouver practice has been developing projects in both Canada and USA. The firm is heavily involved in research projects and has worked in the field of sustainability in collaboration with the University of Texas. Acknowledgments received include the 2008 Canadian Architect Award of Excellence and the 2002 North American Wood Design Award.

## Grande Bibliothèque du Québec
Montreal, Canada / 2005 / Photos: © James Dow, Patkau Architects

This project began with the aim of offering a single site for storage and diffusion for an otherwise scattered series of book collections, and the functions of a public library. With 4,000 m² (43,055 sq ft) of floor space, the new building plays this role to perfection.

The glass-and-copper clad façade houses open-plan spaces.

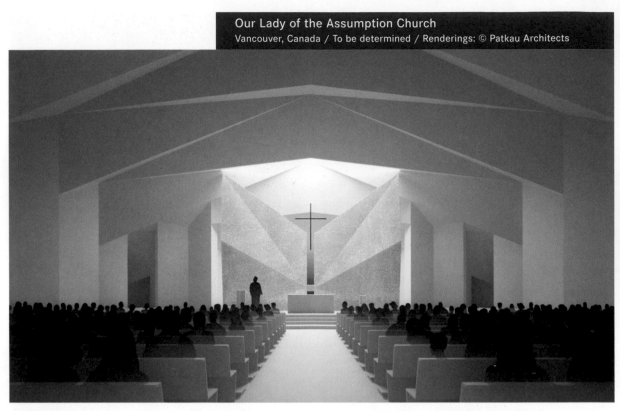

The original form of this religious center marks both the exterior appearance and the internal typology of the building. The accordion-like folds of the façade house free-form interiors.

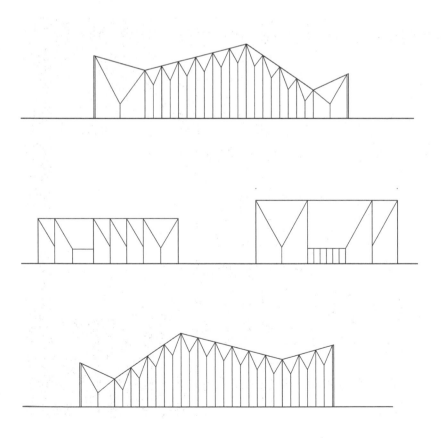

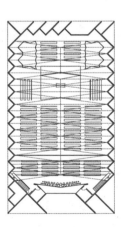

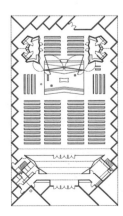

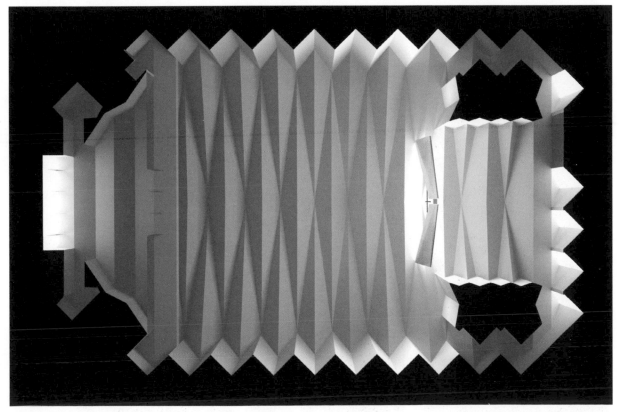

The symmetrical nature of the plan enables the different spaces to be ideally laid out.

Originally built in 1976 as a three-story building, the Winnipeg Centennial Library was in need of major expansion. The architects took advantage of the possibility of increasing space vertically, with new construction consisting of a steel cube that contains the fourth level.

So as to avoid patrons having to go outside in winter, internal connections were improved by means of tunnels and walkways.

Phoenix

## Helena Casanova & Jesús Hernández

© Casanova & Hernández Architecten

Casanova+Hernandez Architecten
Pannekoestraat 104
3011 LL Rotterdam, The Netherlands
Tel.: +31 10 240 9333
www.casanova-hernandez.com

Helena Casanova and Jesús Hernández were born in Madrid in 1967 and graduated from the Madrid School of Architecture. Both worked at the West 8 firm in Rotterdam before founding their own practice in the same city in 2001. Specializing in urban planning and landscape architecture, the firm shows a strong experimental tendency and an interest in the design of public buildings.

## Groningen Villas
Groningen, The Netherlands / 2005 / Photos: © John Lewis Marshall

This residential project features a wooden wall that runs between the buildings and the small outbuildings serving as storage spaces. Its function is to separate the garden areas.

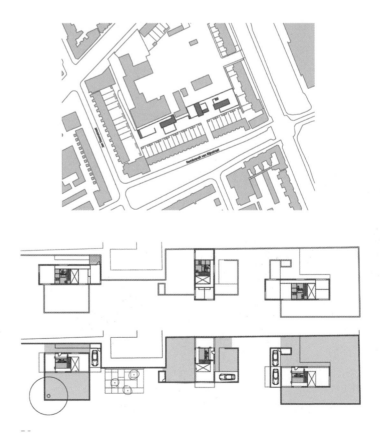

The three villas are brought together by the wooden ribbon, which becomes the main unifying feature.

The strategy, given the name of *sushi à la carte*, is a plan that offers three types of residential layouts based on one organizational concept. A continuous skin with a series of perforations encompasses the three buildings and provides them with a unified character.

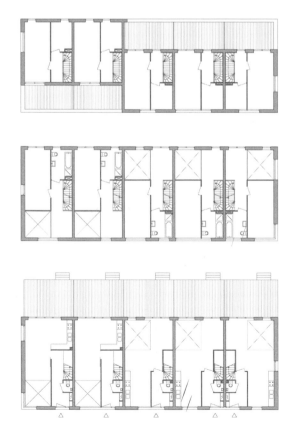

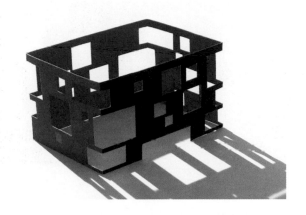

The outdoor areas are as carefully designed as the buildings, maintaining a close relationship both in space and in the views created.

This new project consists of the construction of a plinth that will contain the living and working spaces, and creates a type of agora that establishes a dialogue with its urban setting.

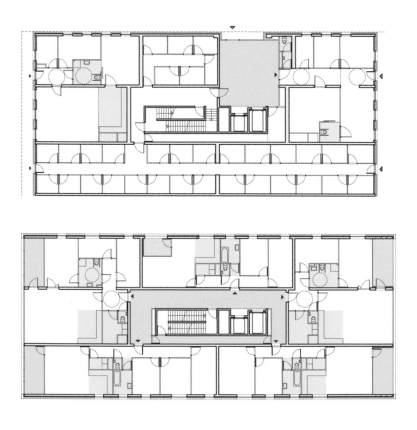

Most of the living spaces are contained in three long volumes with many large windows.

Facing a park, this new residential development has been given the task of renewing the area. The project features a green façade designed with different patterns over a glass surface.

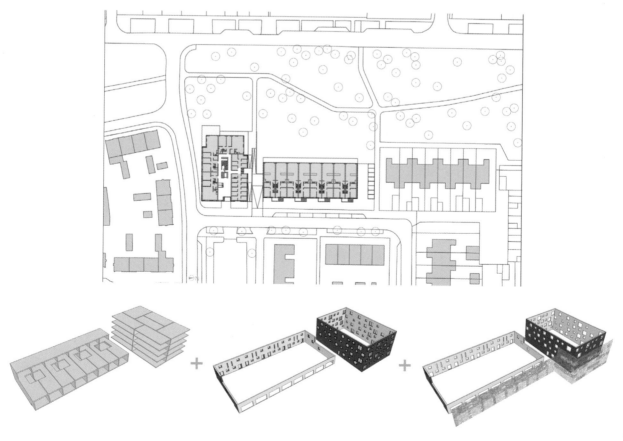

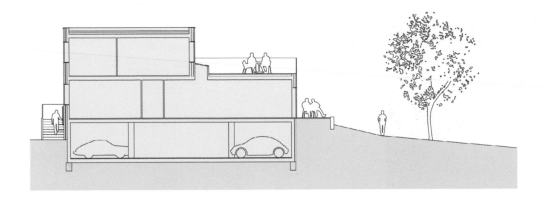

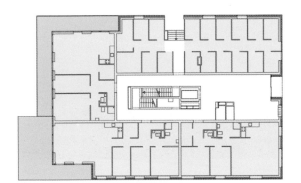

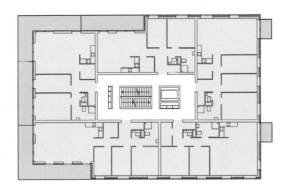

The building features a façade built of stone and broken by different perforations arranged to ensure good visibility.

Apus

## John Portman

© Courtesy of HFN

John Portman & Associates
303 Peachtree Center Avenue, suite 575
Atlanta, GA 30308, USA
Tel.: +1 404 614 5555
www.portmanusa.com

John Portman, born in Walhalla, South Caroli-na, in 1924, is an architect with special renown for the style of his hotels. Graduating from the Georgia Institute of Technology in 1950, he soon achieved success with projects such as the Bonaventure Hotel in Los Angeles and the Renaissance Center in Detroit, which was the tallest hotel in the world when built in 1977. Acknowledgments he has received include the AIA Medal for Innovations in Hotel Design and the Urban Land Institute Award of Excellence for the Embarcadero Center project in San Francisco, California.

## Beijing Yintai Centre
Beijing, China / 2008 / Photos: © Courtesy of Beijing Yintai Centre, Park Hyatt Beijing

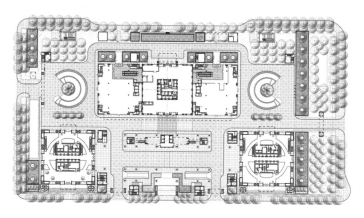

This mixed-use development features a 250 m (820 ft) central tower housing a hotel and luxury residences, and two office towers rising 186 m (610 ft) in height. With a total of 63 floors and four basement levels, the complex has a total floor space of 32,000 m² (344,500 sq ft), and parking space for 1,700 cars and 1,500 motorcycles.

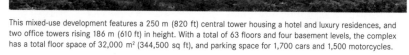

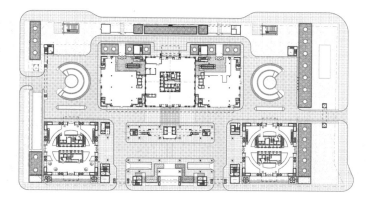

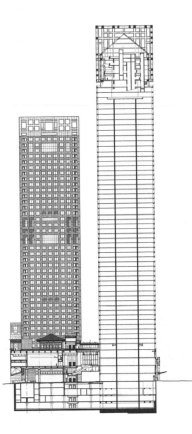

The majestic simplicity of the buildings gives way to the light projected onto the façade at night.

This hotel and convention center has 500 rooms and conference facilities covering more than 9,300 m² (100,000 sq ft). The project master plan also includes the construction of a 2,400-seat auditorium in the future. The exterior gardens are dominated by water features.

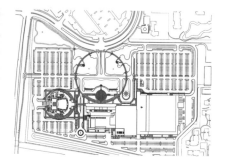
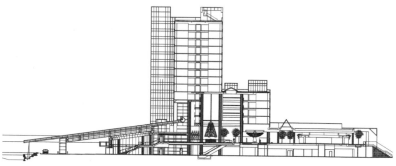

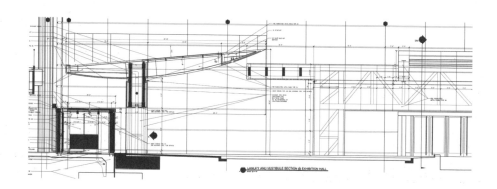

The cone-shaped structure seen here in these architectural renderings corresponds to the adjoining auditorium that is yet to be built. Its completion will mark the finalization of the project.

The exterior of this eye-catching hotel features double curves of aluminum with glass expanses on its façade. A heliport crowns the structure of adjoining cylinders, and the building is surrounded by a landscaped area with profuse vegetation.

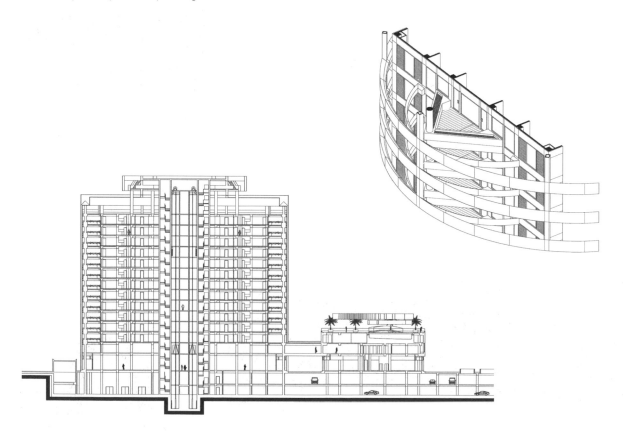

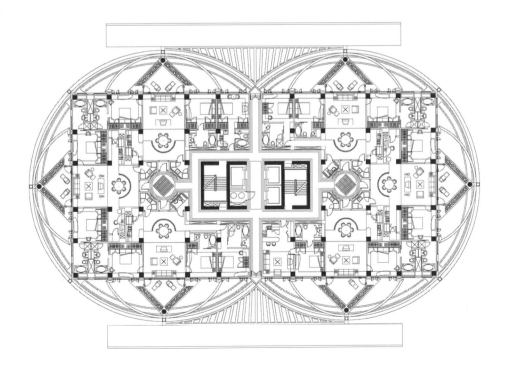

The master plan for the building clearly shows the Asian inspiration behind the project design. Triangular and rectangular forms are contained within the surrounding cylindrical structure.

This building occupied by a hotel is John Portman's attempt to physically materialize the city of Shanghai and its unceasing drive to look towards the future. The slender tower containing hotel rooms and a number of private apartments rises from a plinth where a shopping complex and conference center have been built.

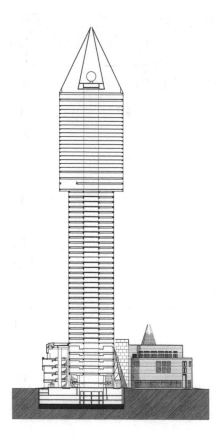

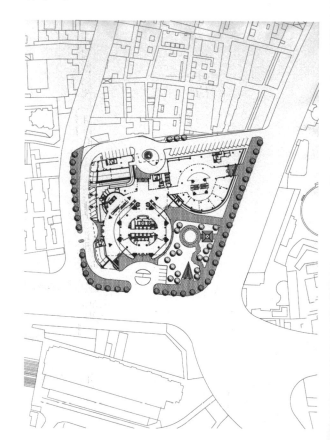

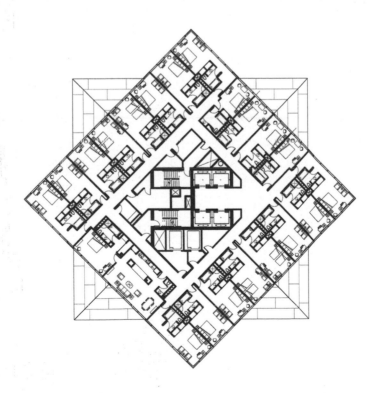

The model floor plan shows the diagonal layout of 20 rooms and one suite around the central core containing elevators and stairs.

With over 360 rooms and almost 1,000 m² (10,800 sq ft) of meeting and events facilities, this hotel is one of the most emblematic buildings in Warsaw. In addition to offering panoramic views over the city, the elevator shaft figures as the building's calling card and distinguishing feature.

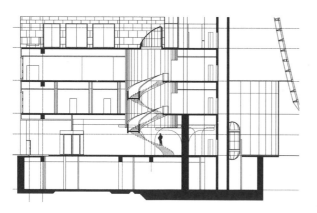

A spectacular spiral staircase dominates the lobby and gives visitors the feeling of floating.

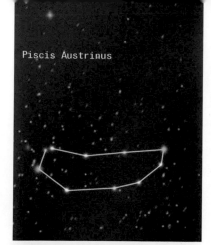

Piscis Austrinus

## Andrew Maynard

**Andrew Maynard Architects**
**397 Smith Street, suite 12**
**Fitzroy, VIC 3065, Australia**
**Tel.: +61 3 9939 6323**
**www.maynardarchitects.com**

Andrew Maynard studied environmental design and architecture at the University of Tasmania. Between 1997 and 1998 he worked for Allom Lovell Architects in Brisbane, and in 2000 he went to work for Six Degrees Architects. He began his private practice in 2002, and in 2004 his work fomed a part of the ADC Young Guns exhibition in New York. The acknowledgments given to his projects include the 2009 Vision Award, a Colour Award for the same year, and the 2008 Master Builder National Award for his Tattoo House project.

## Tattoo House
Melbourne, Australia / 2007 / Photos: © Peter Bennetts

Taking advantage of a very general brief by the owners who wanted to extend an existing three-bedroom house, the architect created an open space with abundant natural light and very high ceilings.

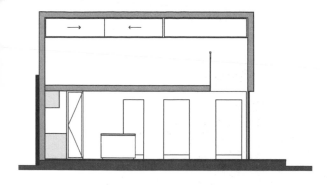

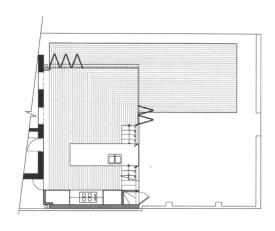

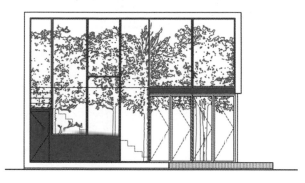

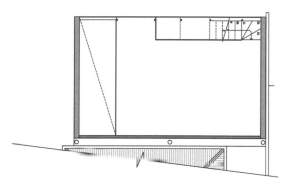

The extension contains a multi-purpose space and the kitchen.

The open and apparently simple character of this house immediately reveals its complex and ambiguous side, given that most of the features fulfill multiple roles. For example, the stairwell becomes an integral part of the kitchen, whose internal wall is also the outer boundary wall.

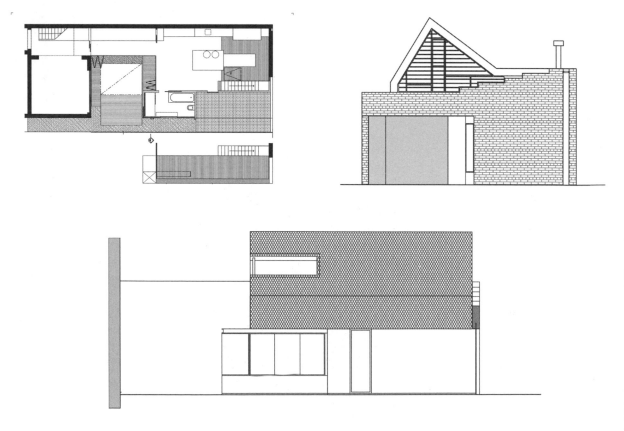

The kitchen smoke vents have been turned into important decorative elements.

## Essex House
### Melbourne, Australia / 2005 / Photos: © Peter Bennetts

In this case, Maynard built a space for his own architectural office, with an exterior typical of homes in this area of Melbourne. Most distinctive are the sun screens on the façade, built of solid recycled wood.

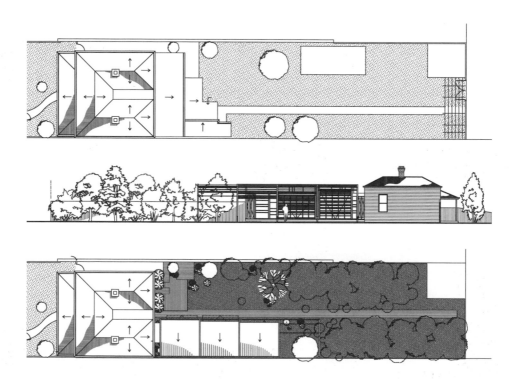

The series of sun screens creates a skeleton that sheathes the house.

## Anglesea House
Anglesea, Australia / 2009 / Photos: © Peter Bennetts

The intention of this project was to enhance the vacational aspect of this second home. This led to the casual style and the importance of the building's relationship with its surroundings.

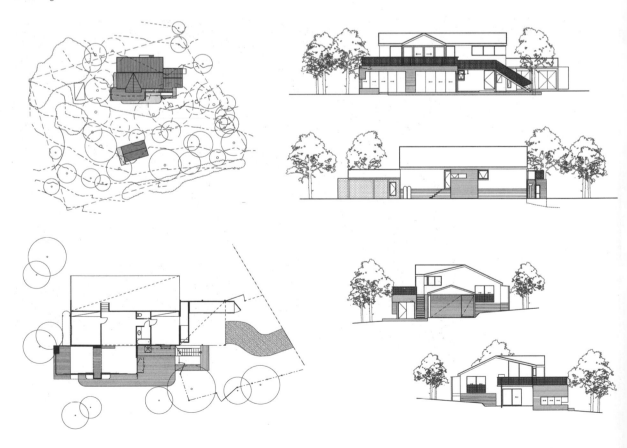

Aside from changing the appearance of the house, the project brought much additional space to the existing building.

Leo Minor

Esther Sperber

© Esther Sperber

Studio ST
330 West 38th Street, suite 1003
New York, NY 10018, USA
Tel.: +1 212 643 2600
www.studio-st.com

After studying at the Technion—Israel Institute of Technology in Haifa—and Columbia University, and working for a time at Pei Partnership Architects, Esther Sperber set up Studio ST in 2003. The studio often takes part in international competitions and one of its projects, Swell House, won the 2008 Architectural Record Award for the best unbuilt house. Besides the winning project for the Kesher Synagogue, Sperber's design for the Prague National Library was a semi-finalist in the competition.

## Slice House
Atlanta, GA, USA / 2006 / Renderings: © Esther Sperber

This project for a single-family residence is based on a box from which slices were cut to divide spaces and create a more intimate atmosphere.

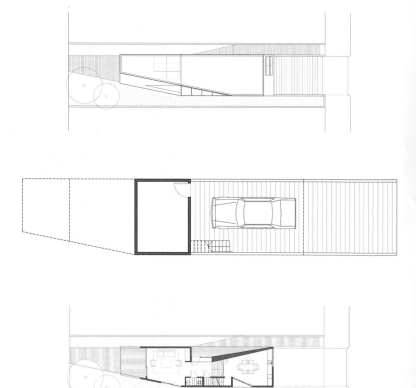

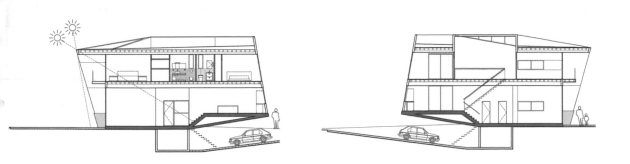

Each of the slices made to the volume enables windows to be installed at points especially considered to offer better lighting.

This new place of worship attracts visitors' attention with its façade, which is clad with metal panels extending like gills over the roof and perimeter walls.

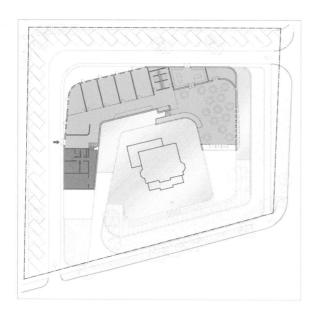

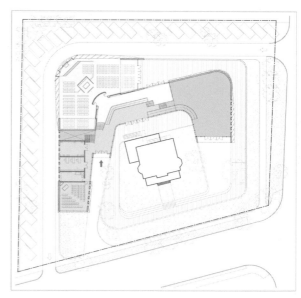

The building surrounds a green space that serves to create an atmosphere of withdrawal.

Musca

## Ton Venhoeven

© Venhoeven CS Architects

Venhoeven CS Architects
Hoogte Kadijk, 143, F15
1018 XB Amsterdam, The Netherlands
Tel.: +31 20 622 8210
www.venhoevencs.nl

Born in Apeldoorn in 1954, Ton Venhoeven is a professor of history of architecture at the Technical University of Eindhoven. He founded Venhoeven CS in Amsterdam in 1988. The acknowledgments received by the firm include a Mies van der Rohe Award nomination in 2007 and another in 2004, and a Rietveld Award in 2007 for the Forum 't Zand project. The members of the architectural firm come from very different cultural backgrounds, and this is behind the diversified approach they take toward different projects, though always with an overriding interest in sustainability.

## Drie Bouwmeesters
Amsterdam, The Netherlands / 2007 / Photos: © Rob Hoekstra

From a distance, the three blocks making up the Drie Brouwmeesters complex seem to form a single volume. With strong horizontal lines, the division between the single-family homes contained in the buildings cannot be perceived, at least from the exterior.

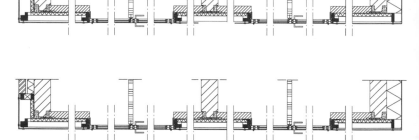

The building surrounds a green space that serves to create an atmosphere of withdrawal.

Musca

## Ton Venhoeven

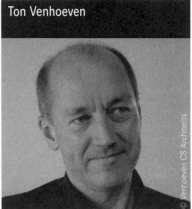

© Venhoeven CS Architects

Venhoeven CS Architects
Hoogte Kadijk, 143, F15
1018 XB Amsterdam, The Netherlands
Tel.: +31 20 622 8210
www.venhoevencs.nl

Born in Apeldoorn in 1954, Ton Venhoeven is a professor of history of architecture at the Technical University of Eindhoven. He founded Venhoeven CS in Amsterdam in 1988. The acknowledgments received by the firm include a Mies van der Rohe Award nomination in 2007 and another in 2004, and a Rietveld Award in 2007 for the Forum 't Zand project. The members of the architectural firm come from very different cultural backgrounds, and this is behind the diversified approach they take toward different projects, though always with an overriding interest in sustainability.

## Drie Bouwmeesters
Amsterdam, The Netherlands / 2007 / Photos: © Rob Hoekstra

From a distance, the three blocks making up the Drie Brouwmeesters complex seem to form a single volume. With strong horizontal lines, the division between the single-family homes contained in the buildings cannot be perceived, at least from the exterior.

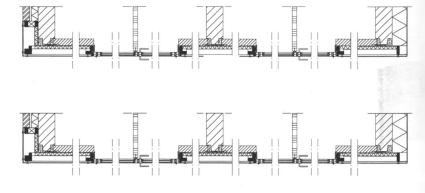

The changing window sequence—in groups of three and two windows, or a single window, provide variability to the façade, which would otherwise seem very monotonous.

# Kindercluster
Utrecht, The Netherlands / 2005 / Photos: © Luuk Kramer

This school contains several classrooms, a day care center, a venue for extracurricular activities, and a space for physical education lessons. The building features a raised floor, held up by pillars clustered in different configurations.

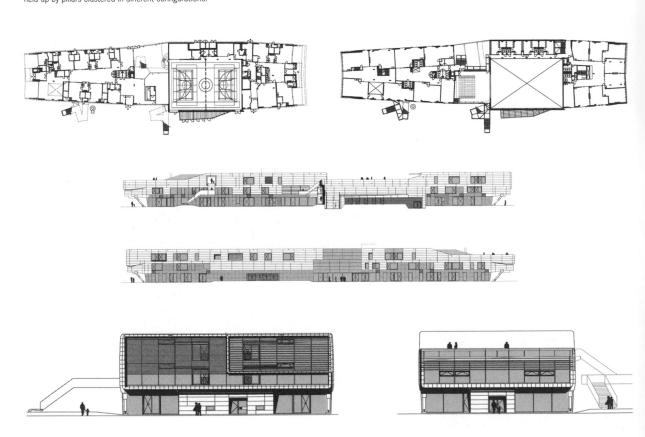

Tho façade displays elements from the old factory that once occupied the site, such as the original chimney.

The focal point for this project is the vertical garden designed by Patrick Blanc. Each plant on the façade grows in its own cube and is fed through an integrated watering system. There are over 50 plant varieties on this imposing wall.

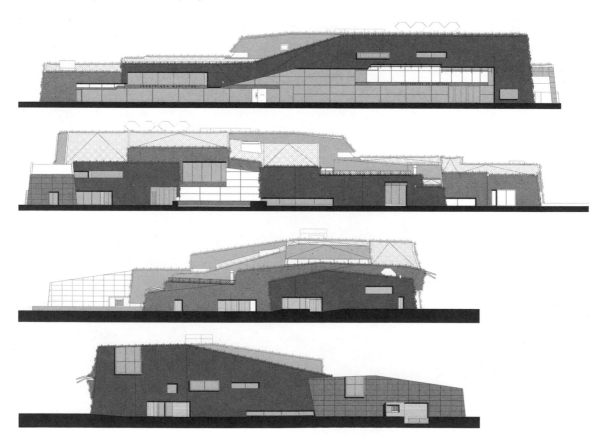

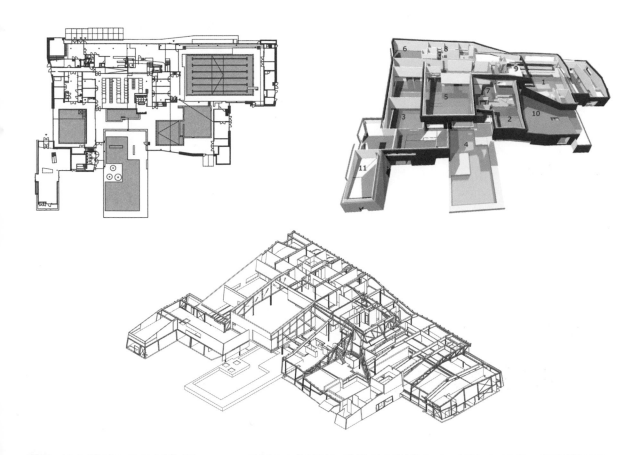

The metal window frames seem to have been embedded under pressure.

This residential tower development comprises 120 apartments for sale and 36 for rent, in addition to nearly 800 m² (8,600 sq ft) of space for offices and three parking garages with 147 spaces. The complex also features a level area where a park has been built, including a baseball field.

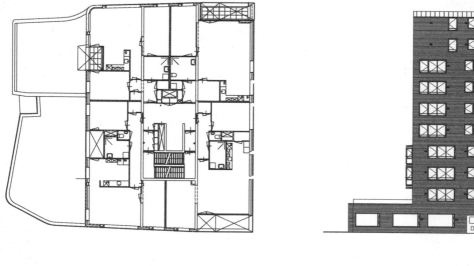

The five towers are clad in prefabricated aluminum panels and contain apartments with diverse layouts.

**U2**
Amsterdam, The Netherlands / 2001 / Photos: © Luuk Kramer

This project is part of a series of pilot projects planned for the regeneration of a suburban area west of Amsterdam. With a U-shaped floor plan, the project features several almost totally glassed façades plus an elegant metal cladding.

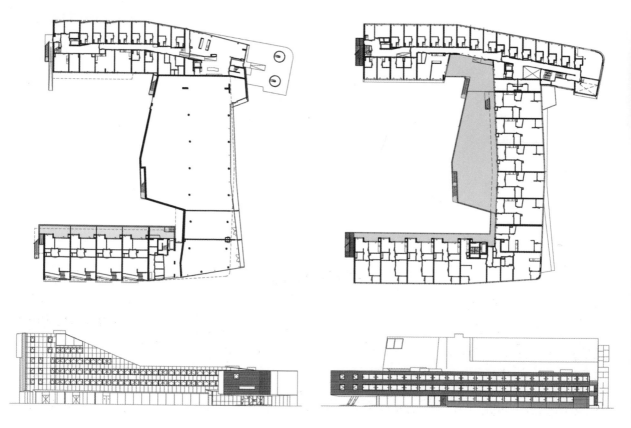

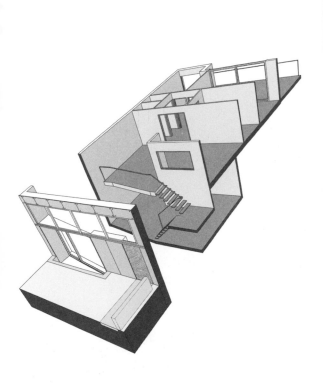

The complex contains 39 apartments, 4 for homes for senior citizens and 50 rooms that are part of a psychiatric facility for older people.

This residential building is located in the eastern side of the Groot Zandveld Park, and contains 22 apartments and a basement parking garage reached either by elevator or through the foyer.

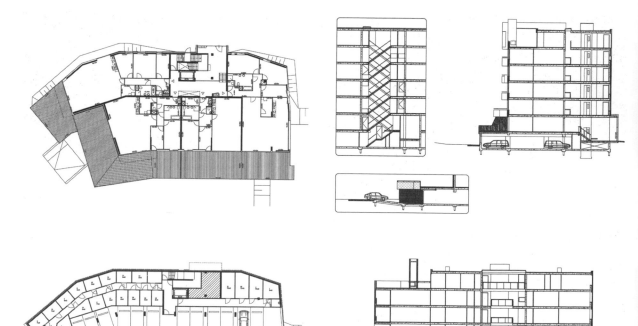

The western and southern façades have balconies and porches that benefit from solar exposure, and enjoy fabulous views of the green spaces.

Octans

## Naoki Terada

© Terada Design Architects

**Terada Design Architects**
**2-19-13 ASK Building**
**2F Kabukicho, Shinjuku-ku**
**Tokyo 160-0021, Japan**
**Tel.: +81 3 6413 5700**
**www.teradadesign.com**

Naoki Terada was born in Osaka, Japan, in 1967, and obtained a degree in engineering at Meiji University in 1989. Before founding his own practice, he worked for firms such as Palffy & Associates and K/O Design. He established Terada Design Architects in 2003. He has held teaching positions at Nihon, Meiji and Tokyo Denki universities and has received acknowledgments such as the Toyama Product Design Prize and several Good Design Awards for different pieces of furniture.

## College of Music
Kawasaki, Japan / 2009 / Photos: © Yuki Omori

Naoki Terada's firm was commissioned to design the interiors and signage for this music school. The project features intense colors and the use of different intersecting angles to create chromatic contrasts.

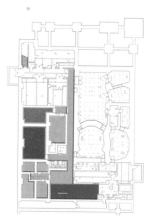

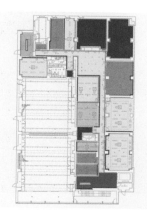

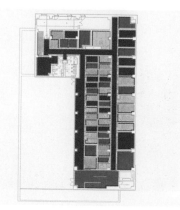

The strategic use of color provides clear separation for zones and spaces.

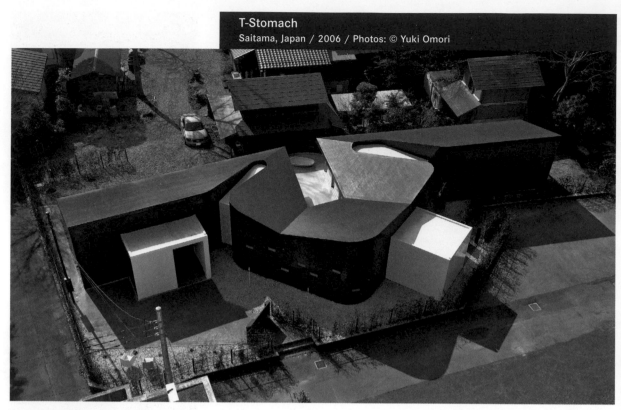

## T-Stomach

Saitama, Japan / 2006 / Photos: © Yuki Omori

This residence located on the outskirts of Tokyo was designed for a family with two children. The design makes daring use of color in combination with the effects created by filtered natural light. The spaces are seamless and flowing, as requested in the clients' brief.

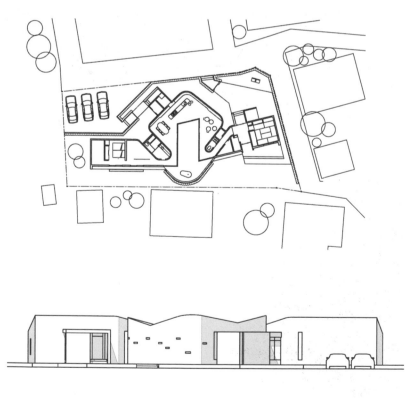

Most of the interior walls are painted a traditional kimono green.

Pavo

Giovanni Vaccarini

© Alessandro Ciampi

Giovanni Vaccarini
Corso Garibaldi, 24
64021 Giulianova, Italy
Tel.: +39 85 802 8625
www.giovannivaccarini.it

Born in 1966, Giovanni Vaccarini graduated with distinction from the Gabriele D'Annunzio University in Pescara in 1983. He held a teaching position at the same university from 1995 through 2001 and currently teaches at different Italian institutions as a visiting professor. His architectural work is carried out in a research laboratory and focuses on analysis and theory. His competition-winning projects include a concert hall in Sarajevo, the city hall in Ortona, and the Crafts Center in Guardiagrele in Abruzzo.

## Arena Braga
### Giulianova, Italy / 2003 / Photos: © Alessandro Ciampi

This building stands on a rectangular plot located beside the sea. The site characteristics complicated the process of adjusting the shape of the volume to the owners' brief. Striking wave-like sun screens on the façade protect the balconies.

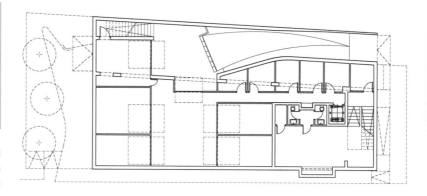

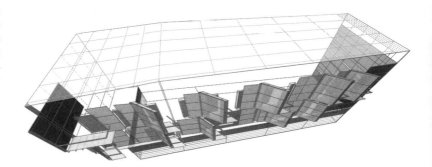

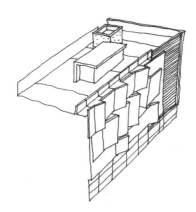

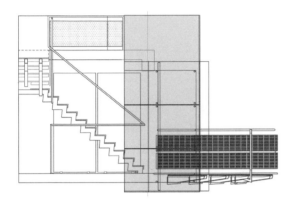

The residences are for use in the summer so a simple design was adopted.

Located on an axis formed by the two main streets of the town, Astra is a building divided into four levels: the basement, which houses the parking garage, the first floor with commercial space, and the intermediate and upper levels devoted to residential use.

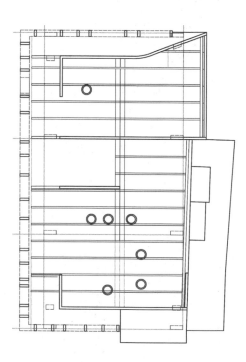

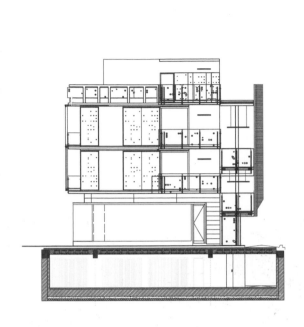

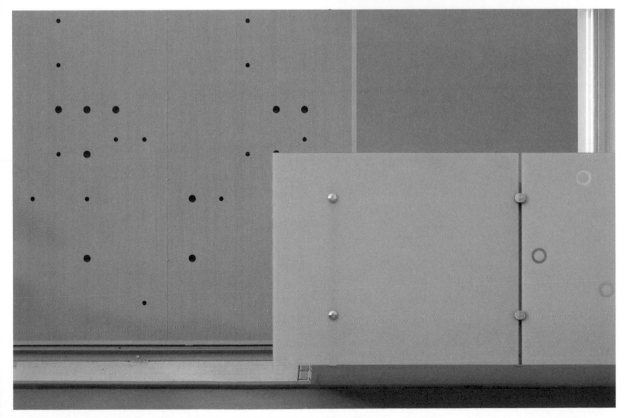

The façade is organized by means of a modular frame that also divides the interior spaces of the apartments.

## C + V House

Giulianova, Italy / 2005 / Photos: © Alessandro Ciampi

Built for a young couple, this home is located in a suburb of two-story single-family homes. The general idea was to build a volume with a back-to-front layout: facing a low ridge, not the city. A totally excavated underground level contains a large, multi-purpose space.

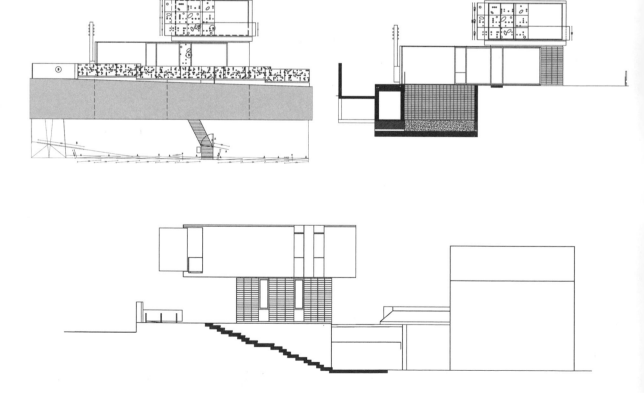

All of the private areas are contained on the uppermost level.

## Stone Cemetery
Ortona, Italy / 2005 / Photos: © Alessandro Ciampi

There was a two-fold challenge involved in the extension to the cemetery built for victims of the Second World War: to make the best use of the available waterfront site, and to dialogue harmoniously with the pre-existing structures. Two materials were predominantly used: stone for wall facings and white mortar.

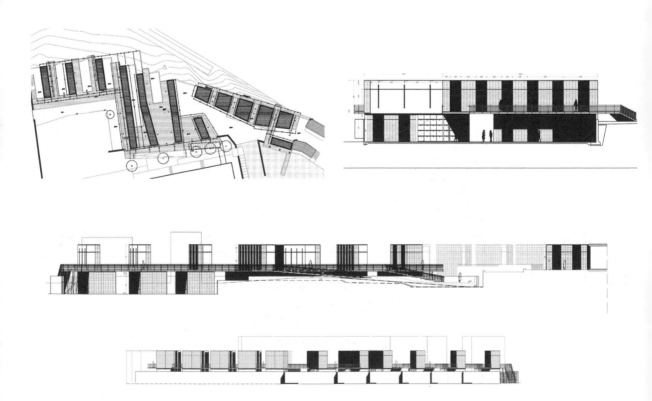

The rough and multi-hued stone was positioned with the intention of resembling a pixel map.

The Racotek company not only commissioned the architect with a building for its facilities, but also one that would provide the firm with a special architectural identity. The result is a project that establishes a dialogue with Racotek's characteristics.

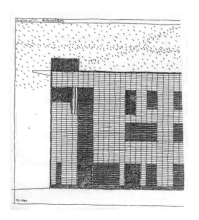

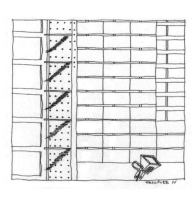

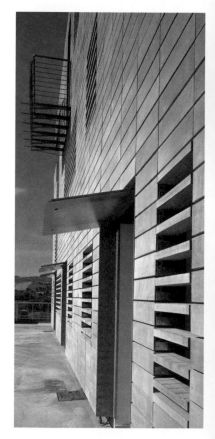

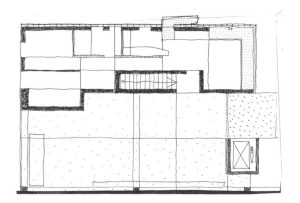

188

The careful design of the façade creates a playful effect between the plan and the actual shape of the building.

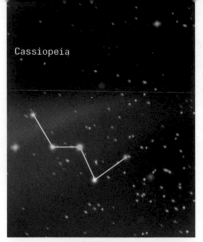

Cassiopeia

## Meinhard von Gerkan & Volkin Marg

© Ute Karen Seggelke

© Wilfried Dechau

GMP—Architekten von Gerkan,
Marg & Partner
Elbchaussee, 139
22763 Hamburg, Germany
Tel.: +49 40 88 151 154
www.gmp-architekten.de

Founded in 1965, today GMP is a firm with over 300 employees in nine offices around the world. One particular feature of the company is that it endeavors to take on all tasks related to the projects it is involved with, from the initial concept and execution through to the interior design. It is internationally renowned for projects such as the Leipzig Exhibition Center and the Berlin Central Station. Among the acknowledgments received are the 2006 Marble Architecture Award, the 2007 IF Gold Award, and the 2004 Peter Josef Krahe Architecture Prize.

## Berlin Central Station
Berlin, Germany / 2006 / Photos: © Marcus Bredt

Located in the historic Tiergarten district, Europe's largest station for long-distance trains has eight platforms and a new subway station. In all, 50 million long-distance travelers and 85 million regional train service passengers are expected to use the station yearly.

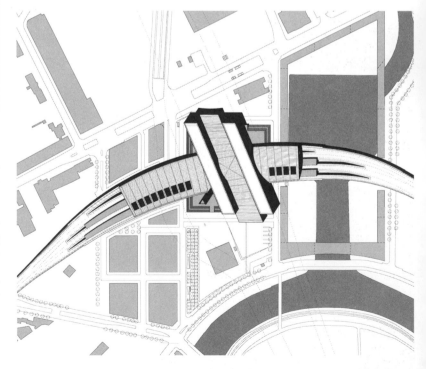

The platforms are 430 m (470 yd) long and run from east to west. They are covered for 320 m (350 yd) of their length.

The main feature of a new sporting complex development, this stadium has 25,000 seats under cover, which were available for use even during the earliest stages of construction. This particularity of execution by stages has influenced many of the characteristics of the project.

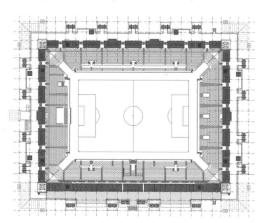

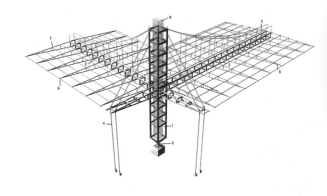

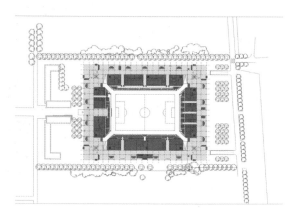

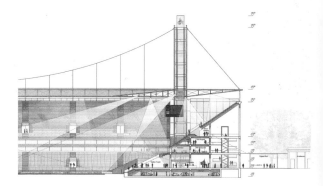

There is a total capacity of 46,000 spectators, with 50 VIP boxes, a press center, and a restaurant.

## Zhongguancun Cultural Center
### Beijing, China / 2006 / Photos: © Christian Gahl

The project for the new Zhongguancun telecommunications tower is a clear example of resource effectiveness and economy. An outstanding part of the design was reflecting the notion of telecommunications on the façade of the building by means of an intelligent system of changing lights.

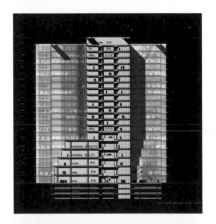

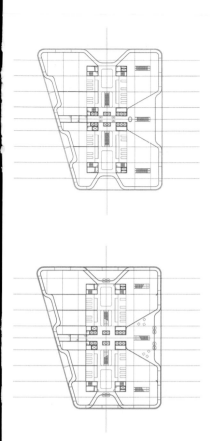

The public areas of the building house two levels of commercial galleries, which are largely accessed from a plaza to the north.

## Guna Villa
Jurmala, Latvia / 2007 / Photos: © Heiner Leiska

The main feature of this villa is not function, rather it is the experience of space that it provides. This residence draws largely from the school of modernism. The living spaces face east, with varying levels depending on the ramps connecting them.

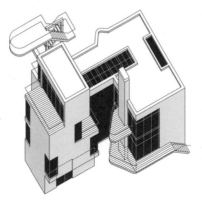

Two large floor-to-ceiling windows connect the interior with the vegetation outside.

This prime example of religious architecture, the largest Christian church in China, has a curved form enhanced by the randomness of its outline. The outer skin of the volume is an organic and uniform layer, only interrupted by the cross that identifies the purpose of the building.

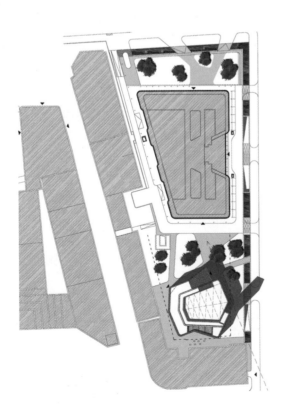

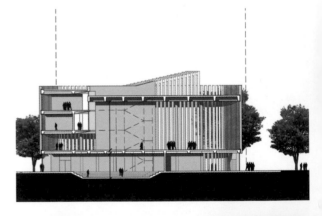

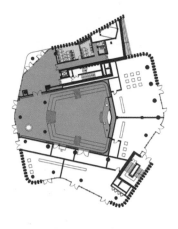

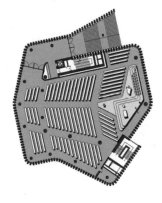

Some of the upper-level spaces overlook a broad terrace (instead of a courtyard) that offers worshippers a distinct exterior space.

At 160 m (200 ft) high and with a floor area of over 89,000 m² (958,000 sq ft), this tower graces the Ningbo skyline with 36 floors occupied by offices, retail galleries, and a five-star Marriott Hotel.

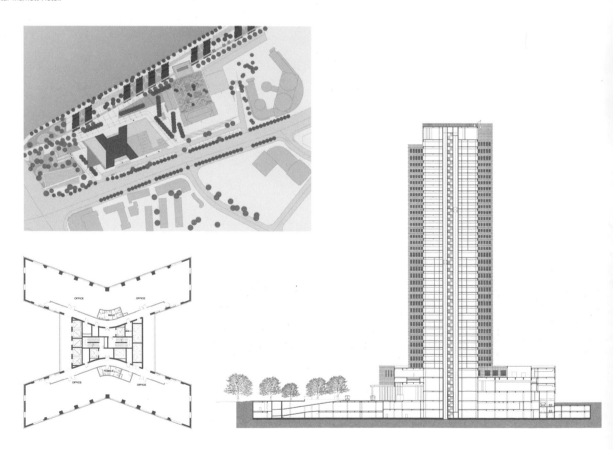

Two curved elements connected in their center give the building a butterfly shape.

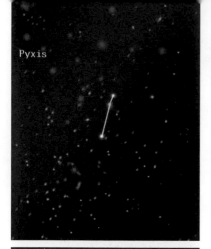

Pyxis

Reinald Top, Rein Jansma,
Rob Torsing & Moshé Zwarts

© Zwarts & Jansma Architects

**Zwarts & Jansma Architects**
**Vijzelstraat 72, Postbus 2129**
**1000 CC Amsterdam, The Netherlands**
**Tel.: +31 20 535 22 00**
**www.zwarts.jansma.nl**

Moshé Zwarts and Rein Jansma founded an architectural practice shortly before 1990. Moshé Zwarts had previously had a long career as a professor at universities in Eindhoven and Delft. Both are currently directors of the firm together with Reinald Top and Rob Torsing. Acknowledgments recently received by the firm include the Routepluim Award for the Beatrixkwartier and the Total Sport Award. The firm has recently received a number of commissions to design sporting facilities.

## Wilhelminatunnel
Rotterdam, The Netherlands / 2005 / Photos: © Zwarts & Jansma Architects

This pedestrian 140 m (460 ft) long tunnel connects the Wilhelminaplein subway station and the Luxor Theater. The tunnel's design does away with unnecessary corners and blind spots to offer users a greater sense of security. Transparency and the absence of obstacles were some of the goals of the project.

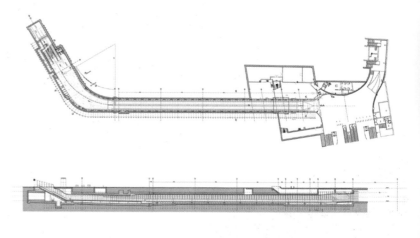

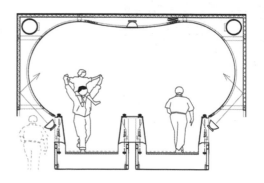

The computer-controlled tunnel illumination gradually changes color.

The Randstadrail project is bringing a new light-rail network to The Hague. A connection between this network and the Dutch Railways station was necessary in the Beatrixkwartier district: this project is for the connecting viaduct. The tubular viaduct 400 m (1,310 ft) in length was built with a skeleton of steel rings, each 10 m (33 ft) in diameter.

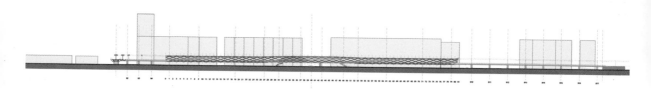

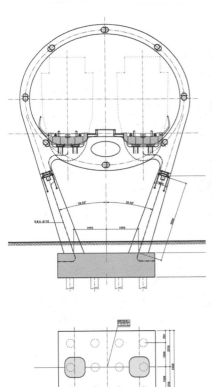

V-shaped columns support the structure containing the two tracks for circulating trains.

Ara

## Kengo Kuma

© Dbox

**Kengo Kuma & Associates**
**2-24-8 BY-CUBE 2F Minami Aoyama**
**Minato-ku, Tokyo 107-0062, Japan**
**Tel.: +81 3 3401 7721**
**www.kkaa.co.jp**

Kengo Kuma, born in Kanagawa, Japan, in 1954, is one of the most internationally-renowned Japanese architects. Graduating from the University of Tokyo in 1979, he completed his studies at Columbia University between 1985 and 1986. He is passionate about traditional Japanese architecture, which he aims to regain and modernize with many of his projects. His works feature imposing façades with relatively unconventional materials, and show his interest in nature. Kuma has taught at the Keio University and has received many awards, such as the 2007 Detail Prize and the 1997 AIA DuPont.

## Z58
Shanghai, China / 2006 / Photos: © Mitsumasa Fujitsuka

So as to connect the building visually with a landscaped setting, the most characteristic strategy of this project was to fix long stainless-steel planter boxes along the façade like the slats of a louver. The end result is amazing integration with the landscape.

The top floor features four glass boxes containing guest rooms, a garden, and an aluminum pergola protecting the terrace.

The challenge faced in this project was to embody the properties of very porous stone from the Ooya quarry with a welcoming architecture that conveyed warmth. To achieve this, a construction system was designed where stones were paired and positioned to give a wicker- like effect.

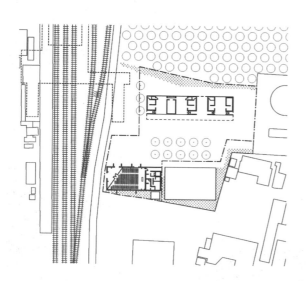

What is really spectacular about the building is that the stone is not only a material that is applied or used as a facing, it is actually a structural component of the walls.

This luminous box overlooks the street through a bold façade made from thin sheets of Pakistani onyx assembled between two glass panels. The façade also features PET panels with a pattern that is very similar to the onyx.

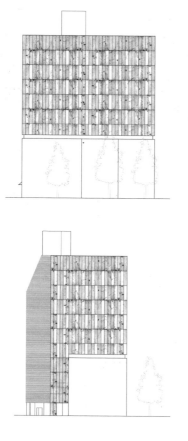

The foyer is lined with the same translucent panels imitating the onyx. Their combination with the shiny steel doors is spectacular.

The typical architecture of the Yusuhara region predominantly features the use of Japanese cedar wood. This was a determining factor in the nature of the town hall project design. The low temperatures reached in the area were also a reason for creating the large atrium.

The incredible thing about the project is the way the framework of cedar beams visibly supports the weight of the enormous volume.

The intention of this project was to offer a cultural space that evoked the same feelings of warmth and comfort as the interiors of traditional Japanese homes with their tatamis and noble wood paneling, in contrast with the bustling city surrounding the site.

Key to achieving the atmosphere of tranquility present in the interior spaces is the carefully-designed lighting. Also adding to this are wooden interior finishes, a reflection of the vertical lines of the façade.

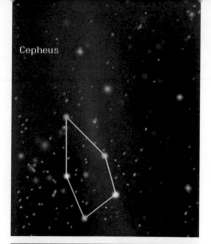

Cepheus

## Lise Anne Couture
## & Hani Rashid

© Alex Cao

**Asymptote Architecture**
**11-45 46th Avenue**
**New York, NY 11101, USA**
**Tel.: +1 212 343 7333**
**www.asymptote.net**

Lise Anne Couture and Hani Rashid founded Asymptote in 1989. From its beginnings, the practice has been outstanding in its implementation of technological innovations in its projects, and for the visionary design of its buildings, art installations, and digital environments. Winners of the 2004 Frederick Kiesler Prize, Lise Anne Couture and Hani Rashid are currently embarking on a series of major projects around the world, such as the Guggenheim Museum in Guadalajara, Mexico, and the Dubai International Financial Center, a 146-story tower.

## Guggenheim Contemporary Art Pavilions
Abu Dhabi, United Arab Emirates / To be determined / Renderings: © Asymptote

These pavilions are two of the 19 spaces commissioned to form the Biennale Park complex, located next to a 1.5 km (0.95 mile) navigable channel on Saadiyat Island where architectural biennales are planned to be held.

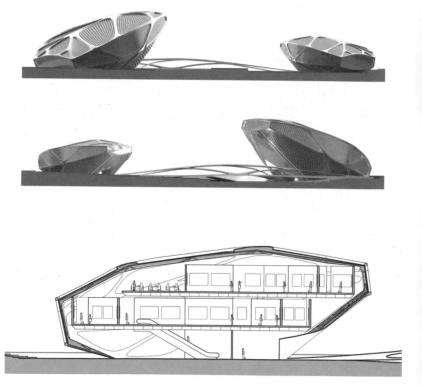

The aim of the architects is to entice visitors into the pavilions through the appeal of their intricate geometry.

These two twisted towers were designed to give the impression of creating a single visual unit, achieved as the result of their respective positions. They seem destined to create a unique image on the Budapest skyline.

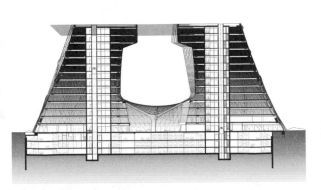

The project also paid attention to the conditions of sustainability and ease of transit between levels.

This incredibly futuristic complex will contain two iconic 60-story towers (with luxury apartments and a five-star hotel) and the Penang Performing Arts Center. It will also include a retail complex and a large public plaza.

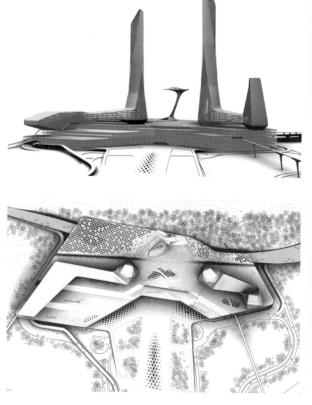

The total absence of right angles is a striking feature of the design of the different buildings.

With a total floor space of 55,000 m² (592,015 sq ft), the Strata Tower aspires to become one of the most arresting architectural landmarks of Abu Dhabi, one of the world's cities with the greatest large-scale development. The tower rises as a segment of a braid, with incredible visual impact.

After five years of construction work, the building will become one of the icons of the city's financial district.

Commissioned by the Solomon Group, this project features a single building achieved by the coexistence of three independent towers. Rising 560 m (1,837 ft), it will be one of the tallest buildings in Asia when finished.

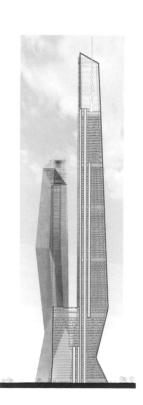

The juxtaposition of different forms in a single building has become the company's hallmark.

Corona Australis

## Victor F. Trey Trahan

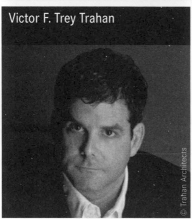

© Trahan Architects

**Trahan Architects**
**445 North Boulevard, suite 570**
**Baton Rouge, LA 70802, USA**
**Tel.: +1 225 924 6333**
**www.trahanarchitects.com**

Established in Louisiana in 1992, the Trey Trahan firm has been gaining prestige with projects featuring technological sophistication and a strong effort to avoid imitation and clichés. Experienced designers of university buildings and financial institution offices, they received the 2005 Architectural Review Award for Emerging Architecture, and among their projects is the Holy Rosary Catholic Church, for which they have already received nine awards. They are currently working on three projects in Beijing for which they won design competitions.

## Holy Rosary Church Complex
St. Amant, LA, USA / 2004 / Photos: © Tim Hursley, The Arkansas Office

The volumes of this religious building are based on the geometry of a tatami, which served as inspiration for the design of the main area of worship.

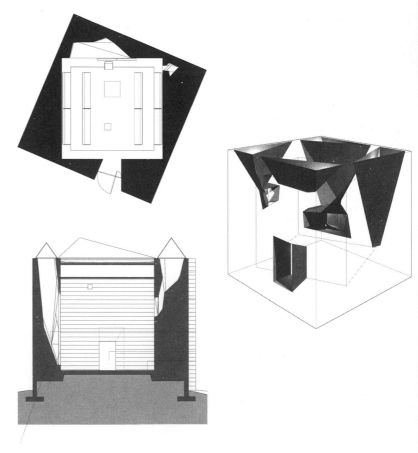

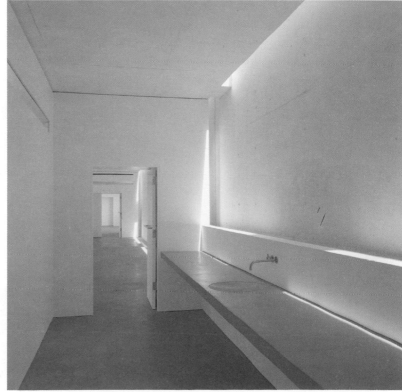

The use of simple and economical materials was intentional, and resulted in the prevalence of concrete finishes.

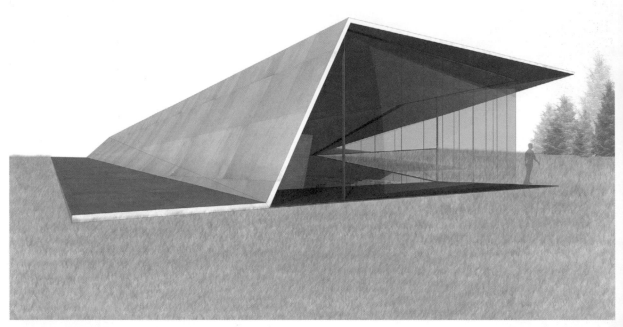

In this other example of religious architecture, the entrance to the volume is found at the apex of a hill. Visitors descend through the slope to enter the church, which gives relief to the site and a false sensation of horizontality.

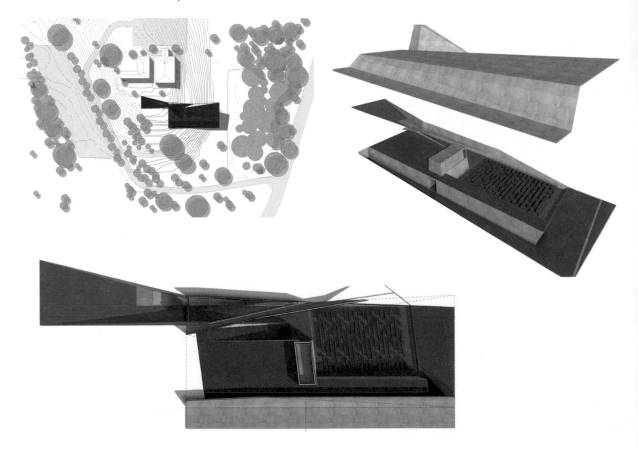

The project features the design of the undulating roof and the spaciousness of the interior, unexpected when viewing the building from the outside.

## Make It Right
New Orleans, LA, USA / To be determined / Renderings: © Trahan Architects

Based on low consumption and safety in the use of materials, this project has the roof as the main architectural expression, since it incorporates the entrance, transit areas and gathering spaces.

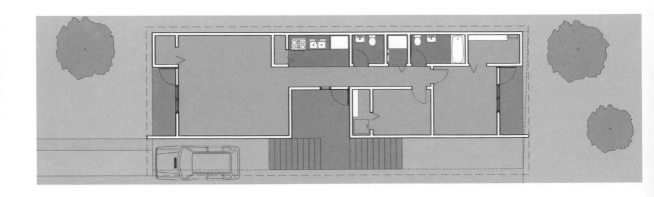

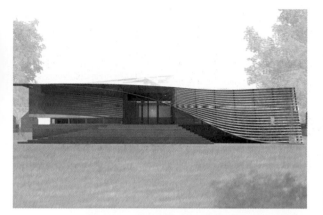

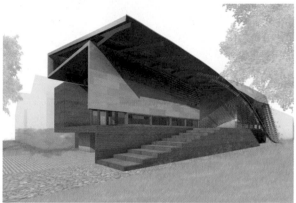

The cantilevered roof holds photovoltaic panels that reduce the building's consumption of electricity.

Crux

Jan Olav Jensen
& Børre Skodvin

© JSA – Jensen & Skodvin Arkitektkontor

JSA—Jensen & Skodvin Arkitektkontor
Fredersborgveien, 11
0177 Oslo, Norway
Tel.: +47 22 99 48 99
www.jsa.no

Jan Olav Jensen and Børre Skodvin established JSA in 1995. The former is a professor at the Faculty of Architecture of the University of Oslo, while the latter teaches at the Design School in the Norwegian capital. JSA has been nominated several times for the Mies van der Rohe Award and has won the Gluelam Award, the Grolsch medal, the Norwegian Architecture Prize, and the Rosa Barba European Landscape Prize. The firm's work has been included in such exhibitions as the Venice Biennale and the 20 Under 40 in 1998.

## Thermal Baths
Bad Gleichenberg, Austria / 2008 / Photos: © Jensen & Skodvin Arkitektkontor

Located in a privileged natural setting, this building features 50 rooms to house patients undergoing treatment with thermal waters. It was important for the sun to reach many parts of the interior, which resulted in the building's form, a network of atriums and courtyards.

The façade is clad with wooden slats to match the complex with the exuberant nature of the surroundings.

Each of the rooms of this unusual hotel is an independent cabin raised above the ground and with one of its walls glazed to offer views of the forest.

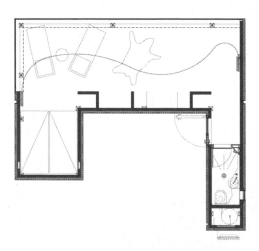

None of the cabins faces another, fostering the illusion that the occupants are isolated in nature.

## Tautra Maria Convent

Tautra, Norway / 2008 / Photos: © Jensen & Skodvin Arkitektkontor

Different typologies are combined in this modern example of religious architecture. The façades have very different finishes and the semi-exterior spaces are the distinguishing features. The project features the use of economic and easy to assemble materials.

The elaborate wooden latticework simulates an interesting coffered ceiling effect, but with the sky as background.

Chosen from among aspiring candidates in a design competition, this project consisted of rebuilding a large Trondheim building after a fire. The greatest novelty in the structure is the inclusion of narrow courtyards.

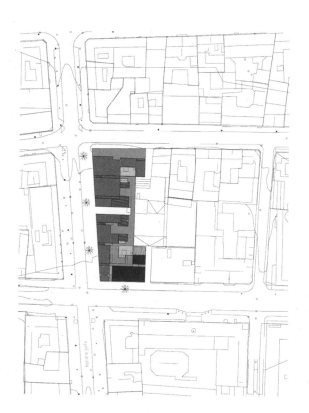

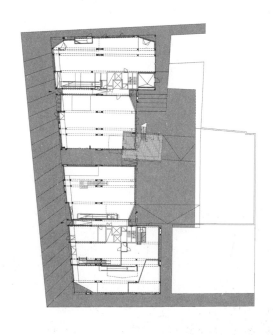

Elegant wooden cladding gives the façade a modern and streamlined look.

There was not enough space on the available plot for a conventional ferry terminal, which is why the adjoining stone wall has become an integral part of the volume when a glass roof was built over it.

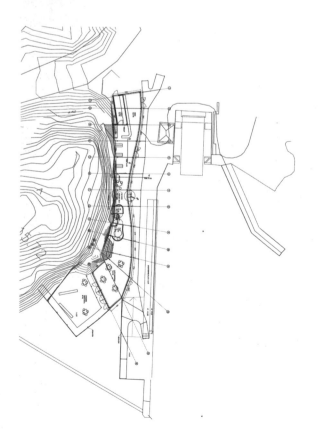

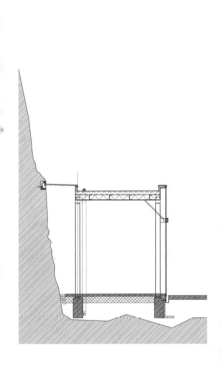

The narrow space led the architects to achieve the lightest structure possible. The result is the predominance of glass.

Libra

Caroline Casey
& Robert Brown

© Penelope Clay

© Jenny Pollack

Casey Brown Architecture
63 William Street, level 1
East Sydney, NSW 2010, Australia
Tel.: +61 2 9360 7977
www.caseybrown.com.au

This architectural studio advocates a functional and non-prescriptive style, based on the organic understanding of building in response to the variables of climate, topography and lifestyle. Among the most outstanding awards they have received are the 2007 MBA House of the Year, the 2003 Timber Design Award for the best design with wood, and more than five RAIA Awards.

## Bungan Beach
Sydney, Australia / 2004 / Photos: © Richard Powers

Located on a site with a slope of nearly 50 degrees, this residence comprises a series of wooden pavilions facing a sunny courtyard.

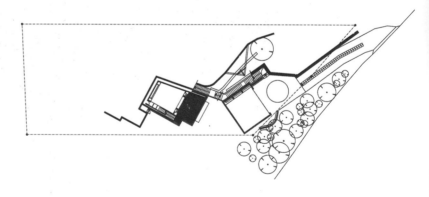

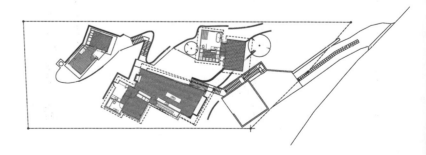

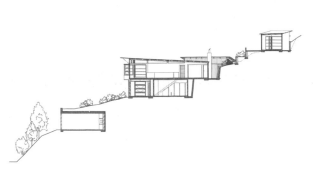

Built at a height, the different towers serve as small lookouts over the neighboring coastline.

## House on a Hill
### Sydney, Australia / 2007 / Photos: © Michael Nicholson

Overlooking the city of Sydney, this Bellevue Hill home is a series of three volumes built on three levels and connected by a central stairway.

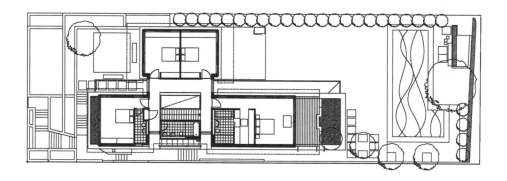

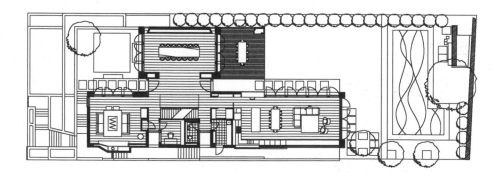

The use of wood is a feature of the design of separating elements and furniture.

Lupus

## Eugene Kohn & William Pedersen

David Leventhal

Lee Polisano

William Louie

James von Klemperer

John Bushel

William Pedersen

KPF—Kohn Pedersen Fox Associates
111 West 57th Street
New York, NY 10019, USA
Tel.: +1 212 977 6500
www.kpf.com

Eugene Kohn, born in 1930, William Pedersen, born in 1938 and Sheldon Fox, born in 1930, died in 2006, founded Kohn Pedersen Fox Associates in 1976. Patricia Conway, head of urban planning and interiors, would join them later. They had all previously formed a part of the John Carl Warnecke studio. With offices in New York, London and Shanghai, KPF received the AIA Architectural Firm Award in 1990 and has executed such important projects as the Shanghai World Finance Center.

## ADIA
**Abu Dhabi, United Arab Emirates / 2006 / Photos: © H. G. Esch**

The key to this building's design is the basic impact the sea has had on the structure of the urban plan. The 38 stories with over 87,000 m² (936,460 sq ft) of office floor space were designed to make the best use of the building's location on the coast.

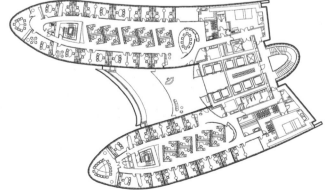

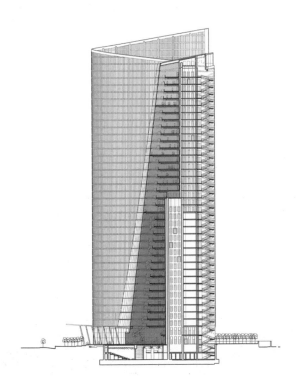

The common areas are striking in their transparency and the organic shapes of the different surfaces.

Located in the Campo de las Naciones business district, this building has 34,200 m² (370,000 sq ft) of offices spread out over five floors, another 24,000 m² (258,000 sq ft) of lower level and basement, plus 1,000 parking spaces.

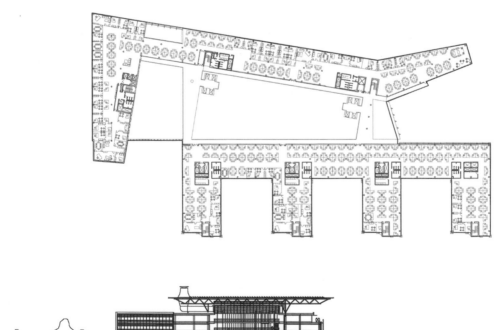

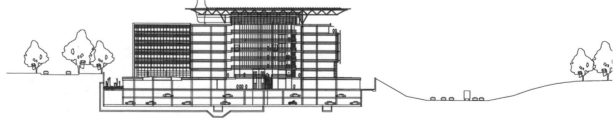

A large central atrium distributes the different work spaces and serves as a reception area and meeting point for visitors.

This mixed-use building is striking for its combination of simple lines and sculptured forms. Its main occupants include Espirito Santo Bank, which has its headquarters there, and the Conrad Hotel.

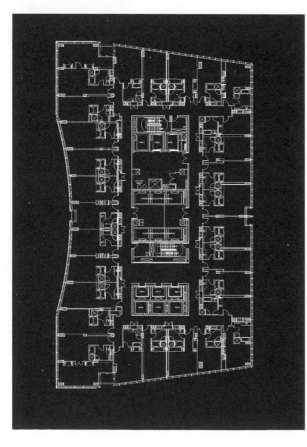

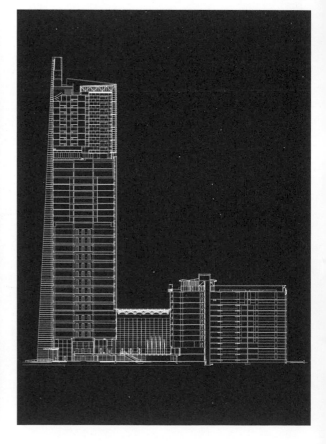

On the 25th floor, a large atrium separates the hotel suites from private condominiums.

A square prism—the symbol traditionally used in China to represent the Earth—this building is divided by two upper arches which, besides symbolizing the sky, give presence to the tower.

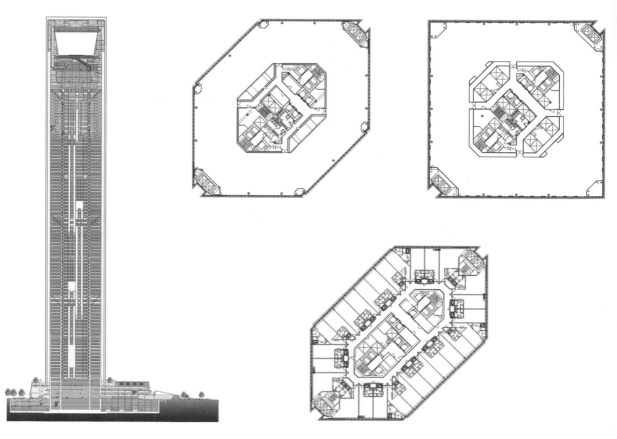

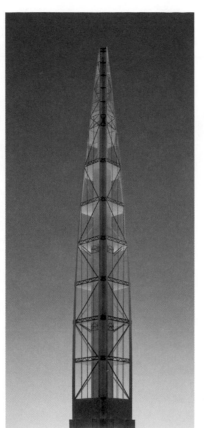
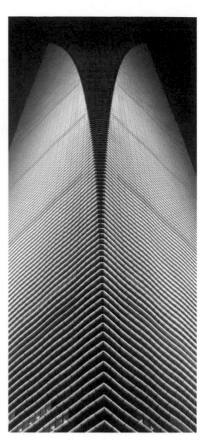

With a total of 101 stories, this skyscraper is a symbol of the area's flourishing economy.

The convention center in New Songdo City is a low-rise complex located next to the main green space of the development. The elements of the site program take form below the visible arches of the floors.

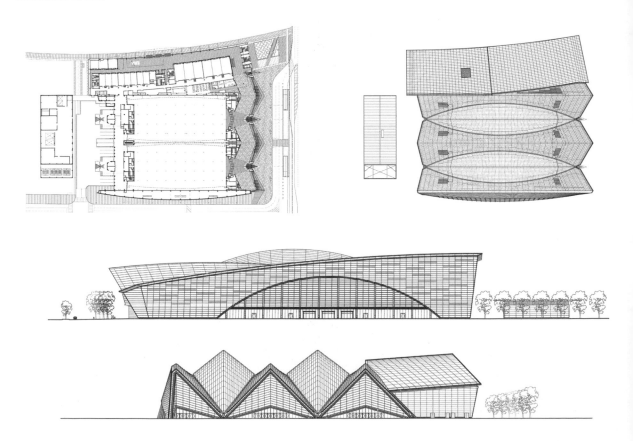

Inside, the roof folds serve to delimit spaces and create the desired feeling of space.

Located on the banks of the Thames near Saint Paul's Cathedral and the Tate Modern, the Unilever building was in need of a thorough remodeling. While maintaining the original spirit of the 1930s project, the redevelopment increases the transparency, visibility, and flexibility of the complex.

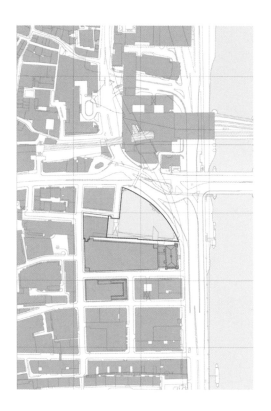

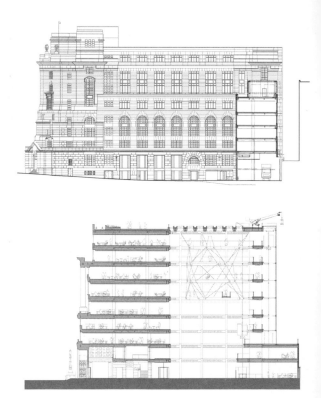

Most of the interior spaces belong to a totally new building.

Pictor

## Dominique Perrault

© Dominique Perrault Architecture

**Dominique Perrault Architecture**
6, rue Bouvier
75011 Paris, France
Tel.: +33 1 44 06 00 00
www.d-p-a.fr

Dominique Perrault was born in Clermont-Ferrand in 1953. He received his architecture degree from the École Nationale Supérieure des Beaux Arts in Paris in 1978 and opened his own practice in 1981. He started his career with the designs for the Someloir factory in Châteaudun. In 1989 a project of his won the competition for the new French National Library in Paris, which was opened six years later. In 2006 Dominique Perrault Architecture opened its first international office in Spain. Acknowledgments received include the 1997 Mies van der Rohe Award and the 2001 World Architecture Award.

**New Mariinsky Theater** / Saint Petersburg, Russia
To be determined / Renderings © Dominique Perrault Architecture

The architect wanted this cultural complex located in the Russian Baltic port to also speak of its surroundings, and this led to an open design. The program includes a large main foyer, a 2,000-seat auditorium and a smaller one seating 350 people.

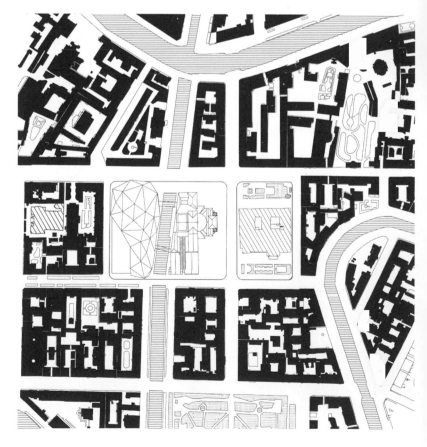

The spectacular "spider's web" encasing the building is the design's most iconic feature.

This project consisted of the construction of a new volume to house most of the city council's offices, with 7,000 m² (75,350 sq ft) of floor space, and a remodeling of the existing building. The new building establishes an interesting dialogue with the older building, which is often reflected in the former's glazed façade.

The complex includes 680 m² (7,320 sq ft) of retail space, built at the city council's request.

Camelopardalis

## MVRDV

© Rob 't Hart

MVRDV
Dunantstraat 10
3024 BC Rotterdam, The Netherlands
Tel.: +31 10 477 28 60
www.mvrdv.nl

Founded in Rotterdam in 1993 by Winy Maas, Jacob van Rijs and Nathalie de Vries, this architecture, urban planning and landscape design practice is one of the European firms with the greatest international projection. There are currently more than 60 people employed. Practical and casual in style, their projects feature a noticeable visual appeal and the intelligent use of resources. Mies van der Rohe finalists on many occasions, they have won the 2005 Marcus Corporation Foundation Prize and the 2002 Netherlands Architecture Institute Award.

## Silodam
Amsterdam, The Netherlands / 2002 / Photos: © Rob 't Hart

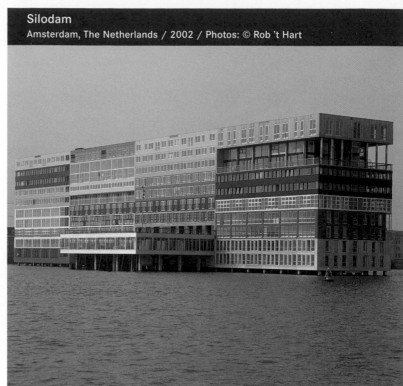

Being 20 m (65 ft) wide and 10 stories tall, this building rising from the water contains 157 apartments. Its shape resembles the grain silos near the port, which were converted into homes. One of the lower spaces is used as an office.

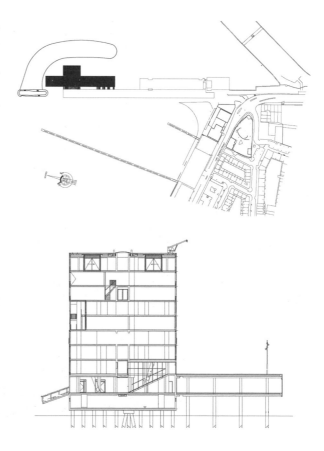

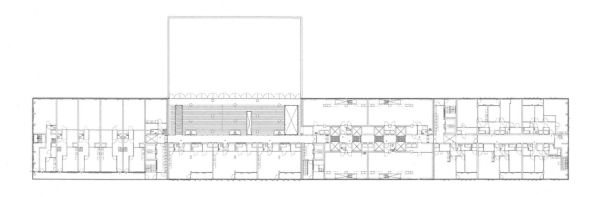

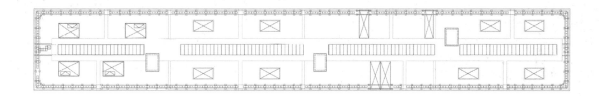

This building's originality is largely found in its varied façade, the result of using different types of metal cladding.

## Parkrand

Amsterdam, The Netherlands / 2007 / Photos: © Rob 't Hart

This complex of 174 apartments is found in the Western Garden Cities development in Amsterdam. Three L-shaped buildings border a small park and create a volume of arresting visual impact. Projections from the façade and floating surfaces achieve this spectacular effect.

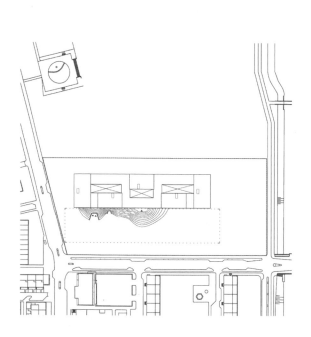

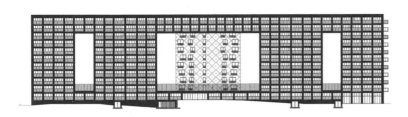

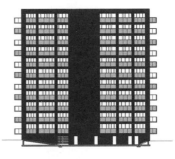

Interior façades are white, with greater simplicity than the metallic gray on the outer wall surfaces of the complex.

This residential building is in the new bedroom community of Sanchinarro, surrounded by highways and located between Madrid and the Guadarrama Mountains. Its 22 stories make it the principal architectural landmark in the area. An impressive terrace 40 m (130 ft) above the ground offers spectacular views of the Spanish capital.

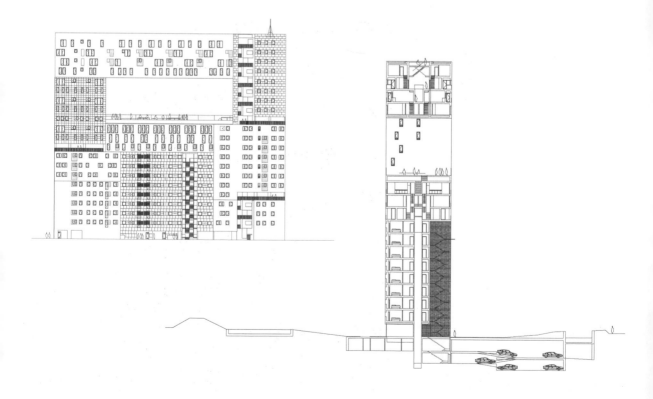

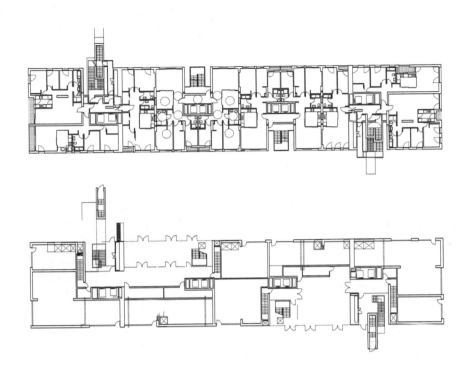

The building, divided into two blocks, has a wide range of apartment types and two identical façades.

This cultural center building is supported by a series of pillars through which access is gained to the interior. These "legs" form the base and create a multi-purpose space under the main volume. The raised position of the building separates the space from the frequent snowfalls that the area is prone to.

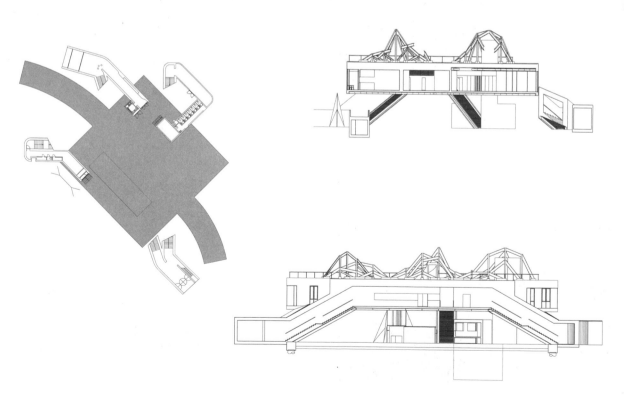

When weather conditions allow, the semi-covered space can be part of the exhibition space or hold events for a large number of people.

This viewing tower was built to regain the appeal this park resort had for visitors during the 1970s and 1980s. Taking full advantage of the privileged site at Anyang Peak, the tower features sinuous forms that appear to extend the spiral path leading to it seamlessly.

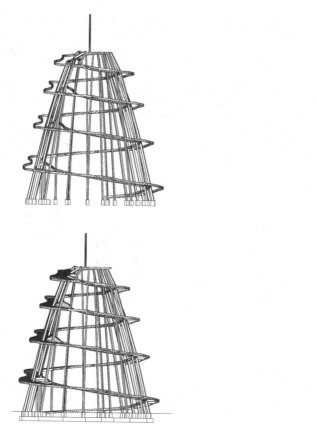

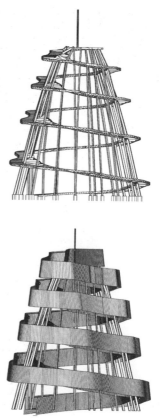

A 146 m (479 ft) walkway and four loops lead up the tower's 15 m (50 ft) height, covering a surface area of 160 m² (1,720 sq ft).

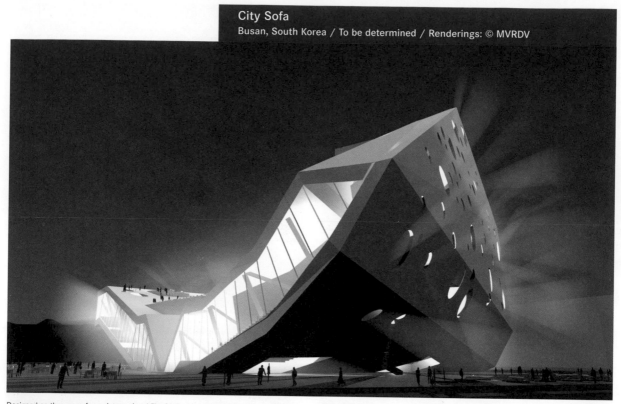

Designed as the venue for an international film festival held in the city, this futuristic structure contains a movie theater complex, a large conference hall, an area with commercial spaces for rent, 250 parking spaces, and an open-air cinema. This venue created was designed with a village-like feel while incorporating all of the items on the design program.

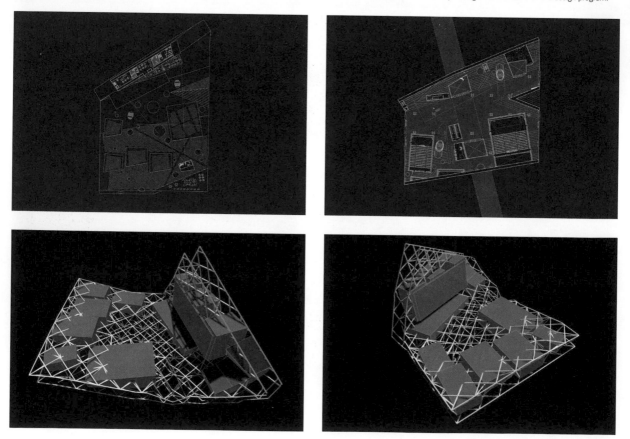

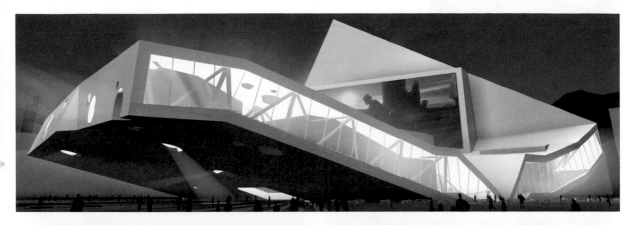

The sandwich-like form enables the building to become a canopy for the half-open space on the level below.

## Robert Toland

© Toland Williams

Toland Williams
101 Sussex Street
Sydney, NSW 2000, Australia
Tel.: +61 2 9290 1944
www.tolandwilliams.com

Established in Sydney in 1975, Robert Toland's practice became Toland Williams 10 years later when Peter Williams became a partner. A commission to design a factory in China in 1987 gave them a foothold in the Asian market, where they have worked from an office in Hong Kong since 1991. Steve Thomas, Renato Giacco, and Chee Lam are among the firm's main architects.

## Pilbara Cultural Centre
Roebourne, Australia / To be determined / Renderings: © Toland Williams

Currently in the development stage, this project includes a master plan and the design of a cultural and community center to house performance and exhibition spaces, and the Ngaluma Yindjibarndi Foundation offices.

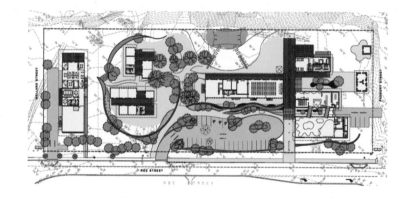

The cultural and community center design was made after an extensive public consultation process conducted in collaboration with the foundation.

Developed in collaboration with Ancher Mortlock Woolley architects and PSB landscape architects, the new ResMed campus is centered on a stream and different green areas to create an ideal space for study and coexistence.

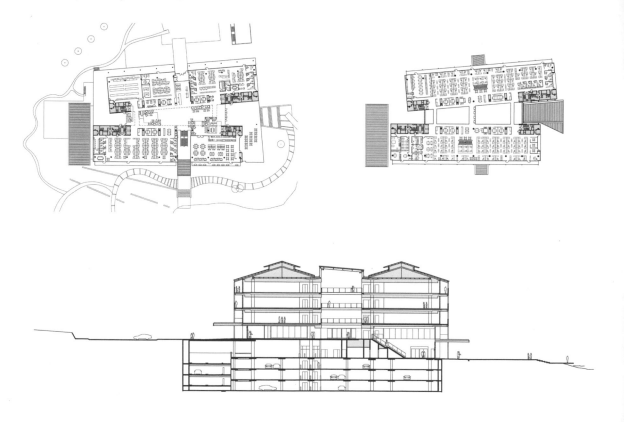

The entire project was developed with the idea of ensuring a high degree of sustainability.

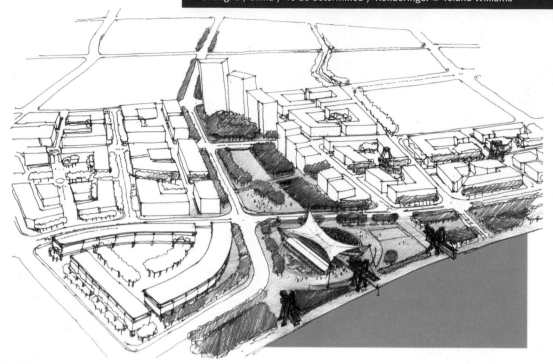

Shanghai Waterfront
Shanghai, China / To be determined / Renderings: © Toland Williams

The commission received by Toland Williams entailed the difficult task of working on an area of 22 km² (8.5 sq miles) of land on the banks of the Huangpu River.

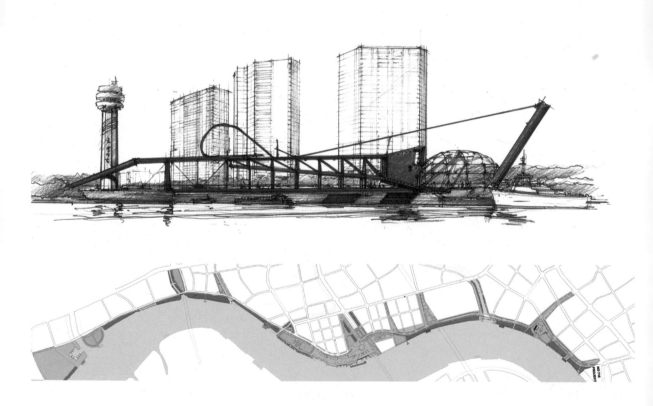

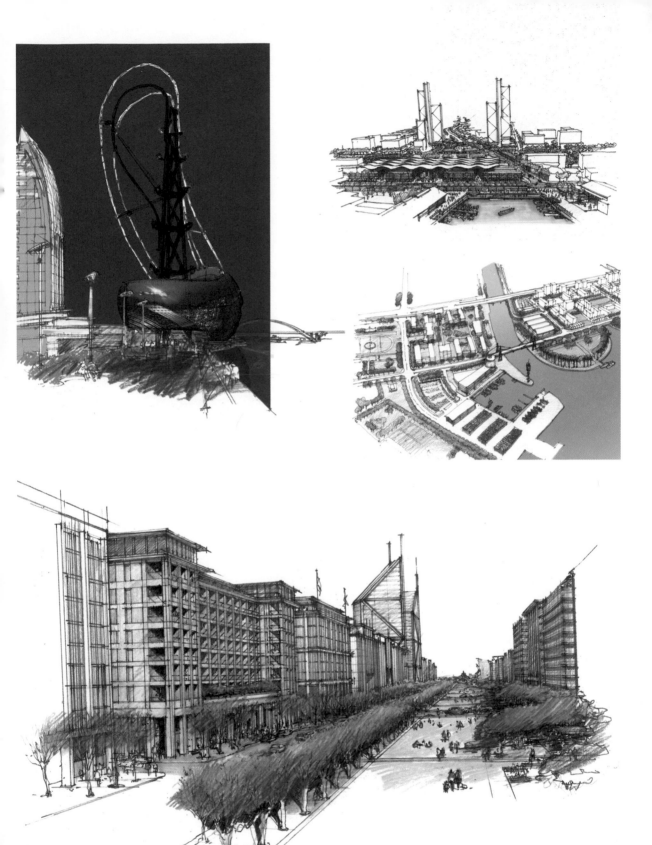

The project includes industrial, commercial and residential areas that will revive the area substantially.

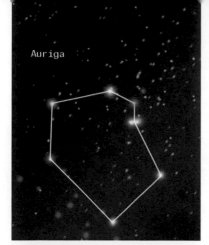

Auriga

## Massimiliano Fuksas

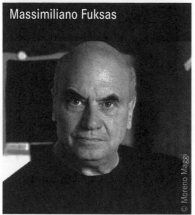

© Moreno Maggi

### Centro Nardini
Bassano del Grappa, Italy / 2004 / Photos: © Maurizio Marcato

The aim of this project was to create a building that evoked the form of distillery tanks with its ellipsoidal glass bulbs. These are two glass bubbles with metal skeletons that house the laboratories of this new research center, suspended in the air with apparently no support.

**Massimiliano Fuksas**
**Piazza del Monte di Pietà, 30**
**00186 Rome, Italy**
**Tel.: +39 66 880 7871**
**www.fuksas.it**

Massimiliano Fuksas was born in Rome in 1944 and graduated from the Faculty of Architecture of the Sapienza University of Rome in 1969. From that year until 1988 he headed the Gramma studio with Anna Maria Sacconi. His firm currently has offices in Rome, Paris, Vienna, and Frankfurt. Between 1998 and 2000 he headed the 7th International Architecture Exhibition at the Venice Biennale, and among his most important awards is the 2005 Italian National Award for Architecture for the new Ferrari headquarters. He is the architecture columnist at *L'espresso* and is an honorary fellow of the American Institute of Architects (AIA).

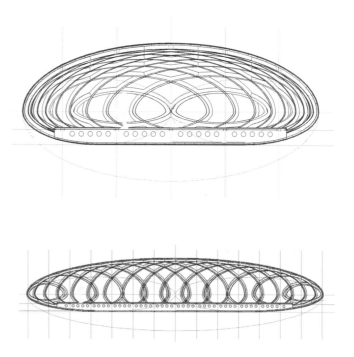

The shadows cast by the metal frames of the bubbles increase the visible impact of the interior. The ellipsoidal shape contributes to the sensation of space.

Milan's new trade exhibition center is one of the most imposing projects recently built in Europe. The impressive finish featuring an enormous glass canopy or sail, covering practically the entire site, makes it an architectural landmark of the city, in addition to providing plentiful natural light to the interior spaces.

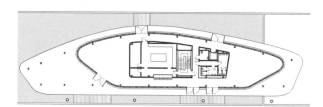

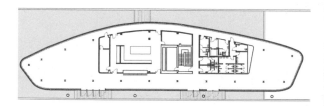

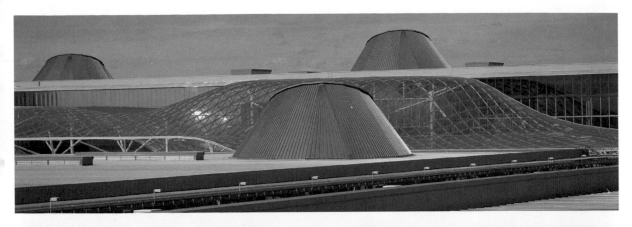

The metal framework holding up the roof comprises a series of triangles connected at each point.

The three buildings forming the Etnapolis Center cover an area of 73,000 m² (785,800 sq ft). The south-facing blue glass façade is mirrored in a canal adjoining the complex. Nighttime backlighting enhances the presence of the building and turns it into one of the most easily identifiable structures in the area.

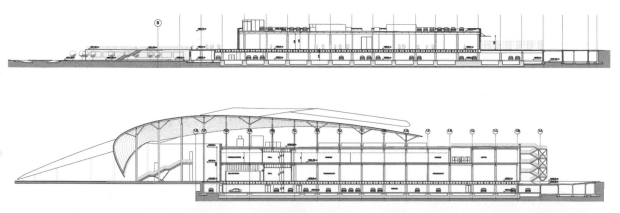

Depending on the incidence of light, the façade is more transparent or more opaque. Spotlights projected from the interior transform the building into a magic lantern at night.

The dynamic design of this concert venue is largely the result of the way the ellipsoidal frame of the metal façade is fragmented and rotated at the same time, in combination with the translucent skin enveloping the foyer.

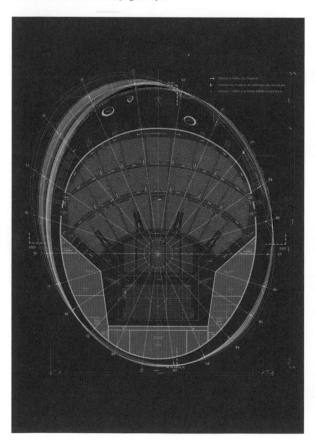

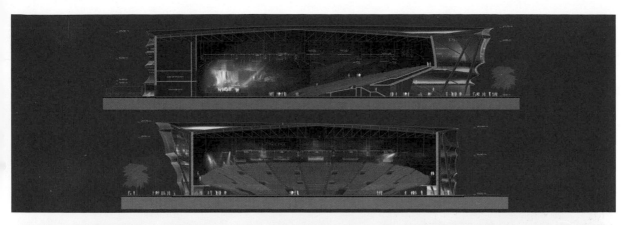

The design is based on a balance between different requirements: good views of the stage from any point, quality acoustics, and optimized building costs.

The main aim of this project was to create an oasis of peace taking full advantage of its privileged seaside location. The building is a parallelepiped that takes shape through the overlaying of glass and concrete. The core stands on a monolithic base.

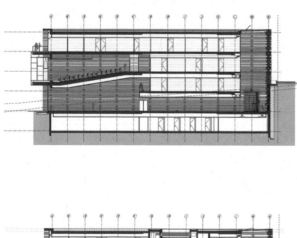

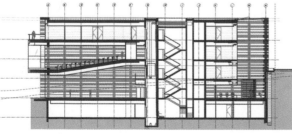

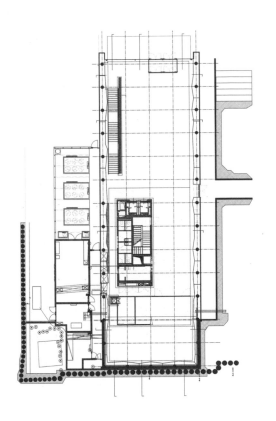

The structure enhances the role of the site as a place for encounter, reflected in the spacious stone basement.

Pegasus

## Darrel O'Donoghue & Dave O'Shea

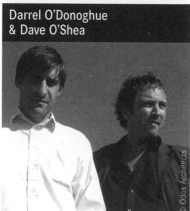

© Odos Architects

Odos Architects
37 Drury Street
Dublin 2, Ireland
Tel.: +353 1 672 5300
www.odosarchitects.com

Darrel O'Donoghue and Dave O'Shea see architecture as a continuous questioning of how to work, rest, and entertain people in today's society. They firmly believe in challenging their clients and in the duty of architects to offer the greatest number of possibilities to whomever requires their services. The acknowledgments received by the firm include an Opus Award in 2009, three AIA Awards (2006, 2007, and 2009), and four RAIA Awards (2005 through 2009).

## Saint Patrick's
Rathfarnham, Ireland / 2006 / Photos: © Edna Kavanagh, Odos Architects

The owners requested more space and light than what they had in their previous residence, which was the reason they chose a house of new construction. The building makes the best use of a small corner plot.

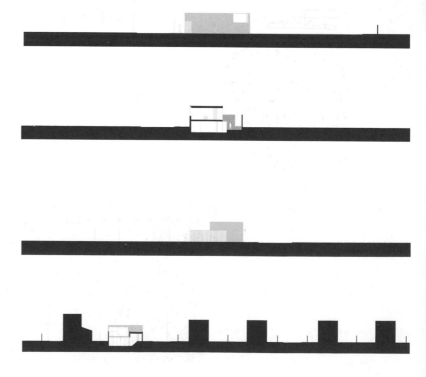

The house has two bedrooms and two bathrooms on the lower level, and the kitchen and other common areas on the upper level.

# Grangegorman
Dublin, Ireland / 2008 / Photos: © Ros Kavanagh, Odos Architects

This residential project involved building two levels over the space occupied by a workshop. They are interconnected by a vertical service and transit core, giving the structure an unmistakably contemporary and uninhibited feel.

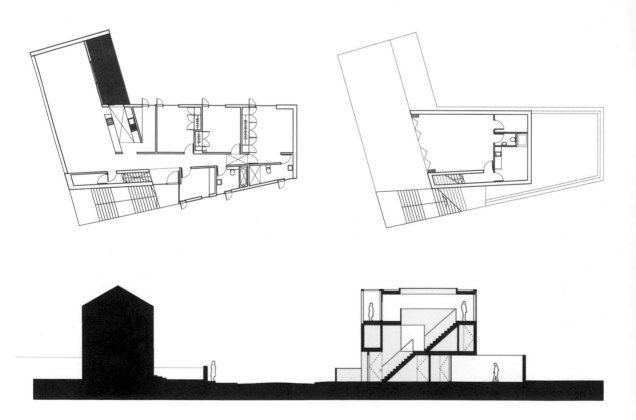

The translucent façade and the predominance of right angles call to mind suburban Japanese residential projects.

This project consisted of remodeling and extending a building occupied by a religious order. The original friary building was left intact, while the façade was almost completely renovated.

The range of materials used on walls was intentionally kept to a minimum, which enabled finishes to be unified.

Built on a steep promontory, the sculptural form of this house is undeniably one of its best features. The lower level contains a two-car garage, boiler room, and a bathroom, while the upper level has three bedrooms, the kitchen, and the living-dining area.

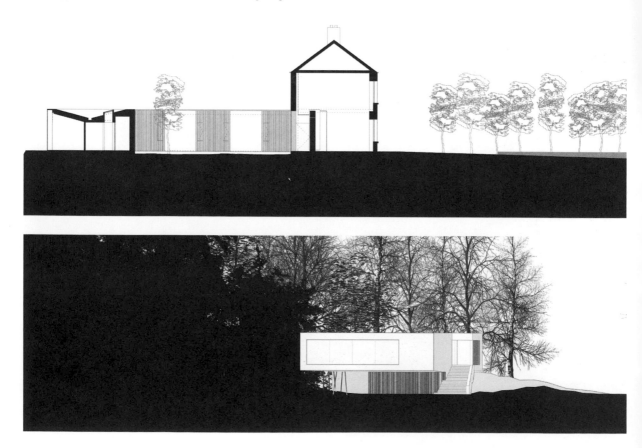

The roof holds a number of skylights, which greatly improve the interior lighting.

The dramatic contrast between the colors on the façade and those used in the interior is one of the highlights of this simple residential project. A solution is given to the limited interior space through the use of sliding doors, which provides a feeling of size.

A skylight that runs almost the entire length of the building complements the evident lack of windows.

Canis Major

## René van Zuuk

© René van Zuuk Architekten

**René van Zuuk Architekten**
**De Fantasie, 9**
**1324 HZ Almere, The Netherlands**
**Tel.: +31 36 5379139**
**www.renevanzuuk.nl**

With an impressive variety of finishes and forms, René van Zuuk's work exudes a sense of diversity that makes it unique. The aim to achieve "something special" in his work, always in agreement with clients, means an ongoing search for the most innovative processes and materials offering the best advantage. This interest in technological development is evident in the general appearance of his projects, which are always on the cutting edge.

## Arcam
### Amsterdam, The Netherlands / 2003 / Photos: © Luuk Kramer

This remodeling project for an architecture center involved preserving some of the columns and floors from the previous structure. The solution chosen was a three-storied trapezoidal building.

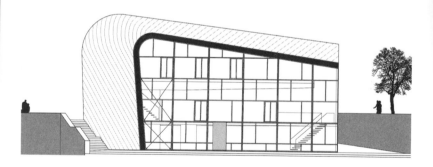

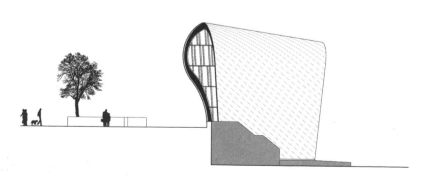

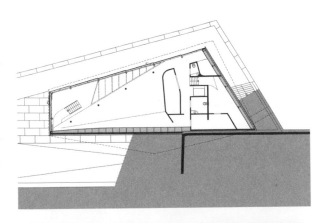

The façade is clad in zinc-coated aluminum strips.

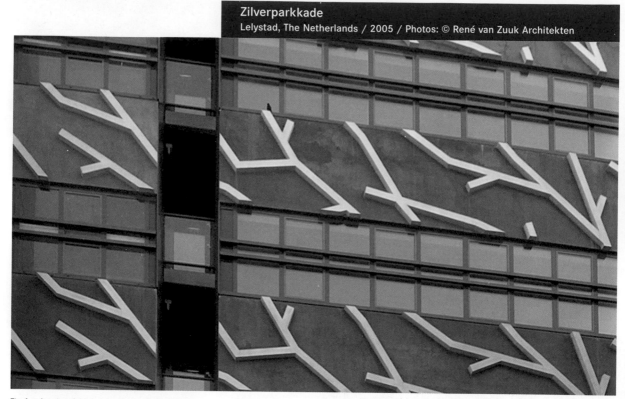

The four façades of this building are totally or partially covered in prefabricated concrete elements that create an eye-catching branch-like structure, inspired by the work of Dutch artist Maurits Escher. This structure was designed so as not to block panoramic views from the interior.

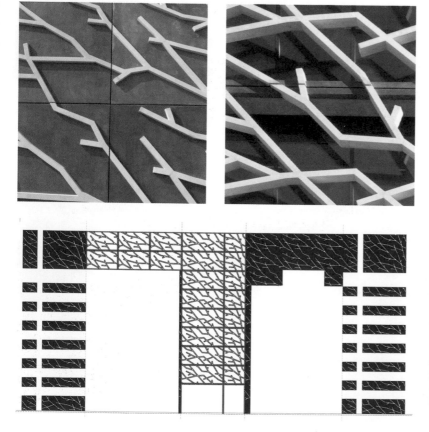

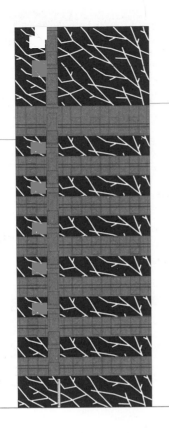

The floor-to-ceiling windows guarantee that the branches outside do not produce a sensation of claustrophobia inside.

Ophiuchus

## Royce YC Hong & Grace S. Cheung

Grace S. Cheung

Xrange
6/F, 51 Heng-Yang Road
Taipei 100, Taiwan
Tel.: +886 2 2383 2003
www.xrange.net

Royce YC Hong is the co-founder and CEO of Agenda Corporation, and before establishing Xrange worked as art director of PChome Online, in Taipei, and as an industrial designer for Matsushita Electric in Japan. Grace S. Cheung received her architecture degree at Columbia University and worked for Patkaus Architects, Bernard Tschumi Architects, and the Asian office of OMA.

## Ant Farm House
### Taipei, Taiwan / 2007 / Photos: © Scott Morgan

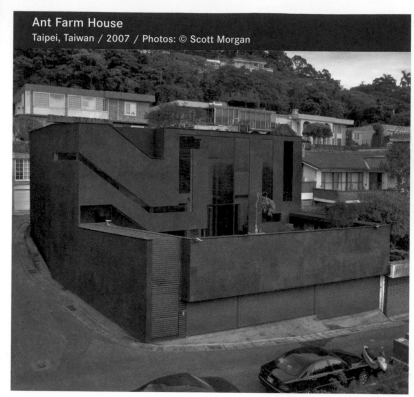

Located on the edge of a national park, the original house was built from granite blocks in the 1950s. As its demolition was not permitted, the architects found a way to change the layout and create a more contemporary façade without touching the foundation.

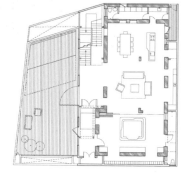

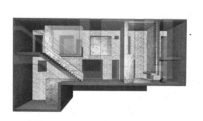

The project basically involved filling spaces around the old structure.

Inspired by the use beetles make of a hard shell for protection and a fine membrane to fly, the design for this coastal home consists of a semi-rigid cell that can be completely closed during the rainy season to provide greater strenth to the structure.

Four prefabricated capsules house the living area, kitchen, bedroom, and bathroom.

**House of Music**
Taipei, Taiwan / 2010 / Renderings: © Xrange

This mini-auditorium was designed as the central space of this home of two musicians. A vertical sound and light channel links all floors of the house.

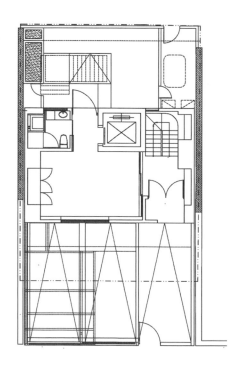

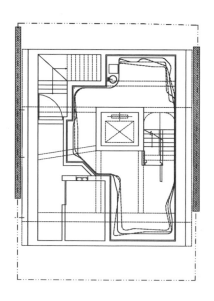

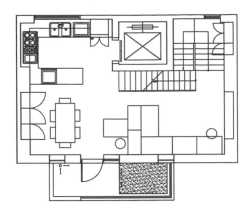

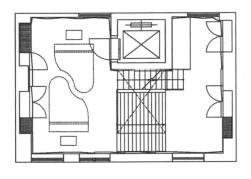

The skin of the building was designed as sheet music, with each wall articulating its own rhythm and texture.

## Museum of Speed

Taipei, Taiwan / To be determined / Renderings: © Xrange

This museum offers a journey through the different periods in the development of connections, from the first Ching dynasty train to the present day. Its design captures the notion of speed through movement, reflected in the abundant transit areas.

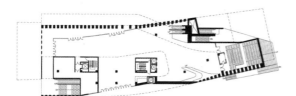

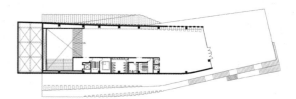

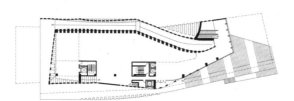

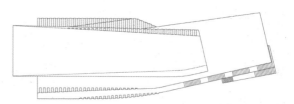

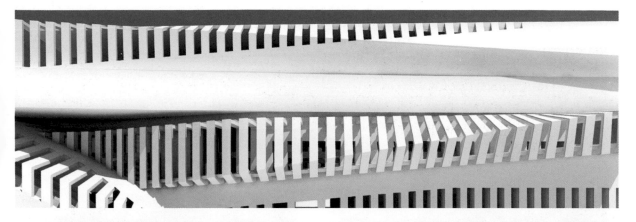

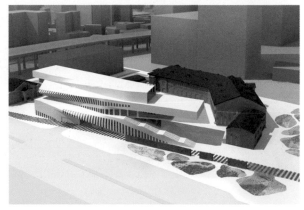

The desired effect is for visitors to experience the sensation of moving through time as they walk through the museum.

## Sun Moon Lake Hotel
Nantou, Taiwan / To be determined / Renderings: © Xrange

The project is marked by the spectacular views of the lake surrounding the site. This is the reason for the balconies and unusual shape of the volume, which offers 360-degree vistas.

The final result is one of a tower raised in a series of terraces that become ever narrower, with an organic form that creates a link with nature.

Scutum

## Per Franson
## & Mattias Wreland

© Franson Wreland

Franson Wreland
Ragvaldsgatan 18
118 46 Stockholm, Sweden
Tel.: +46 8 660 83 90
www.fransonwreland.com

Per Franson studied at the Parsons School of Design in New York and at the Royal Academy of Arts in Stockholm. Mattias Wreland studied architecture and furniture design in Stockholm and at the University of Lund. They established a practice in 2000, and in 2008 they were joined by two new partners, Torbjörn Såthén and Pia Maria. Their main projects to date include the Villa Jensen, a house built in 2004, and Villa Holmer, completed in 2006.

## Villa Holmer
Lake Vättern, Sweden / 2006 / Photos: © Mattias Wreland

Overlooking Lake Vättern, this single-family house consists of two volumes. A continuous wall separates the house from the street leading to it, while the glass façade links it with the natural surroundings on the other side. A spiral staircase leads up to a roof terrace.

A large skylight is located in the middle of the structure between the two volumes, forming a light well.

Several sides of this house, elegantly finished in wood cladding, have few windows or interruptions. On one side, however, the expanse of glass is dramatic and bathes the living area with abundant light.

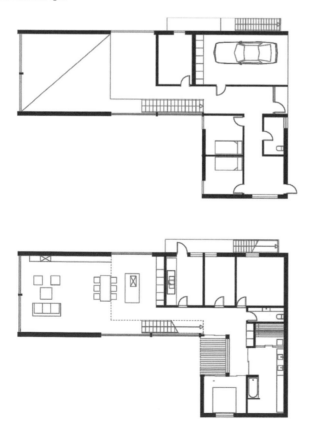

The L-shaped plan provides a pleasing layout.

This complex of 36 prefabricated houses achieved the main objectives of the lowest possible cost, short building times, and offering comfortable spaces despite the reduced size.

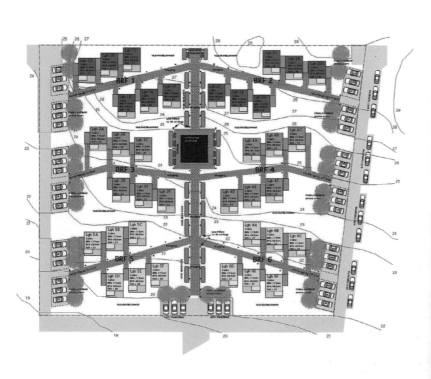

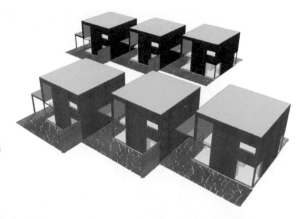

The master plan divides the development into three partially-connected areas.

Lacerta

## Konstantinos Labrinopoulos

© Babis Louïzidis

Klab Architects
2 Achaiou Street Kolonaki
106-75 Athens, Greece
Tel.: +30 210 321 1139
www.klab.gr

Konstantinos Labrinopoulos was born in Athens in 1970 and graduated from the National Technical University in the same city in 1994. He continued his studies in California before setting up KLMF with Miltos Farmakis, where he worked until 2007. When their partnership ended, the studio was renamed Klab Architects. In 2006 Labrinopoulos became one of the founders of the Athens 9 movement, which culminated in an important workshop at the University of Patras. He has taught at the universities in Timsoara and Bucharest.

# Summer House
Andros, Greece / 2008 / Photos: © Klab Architects

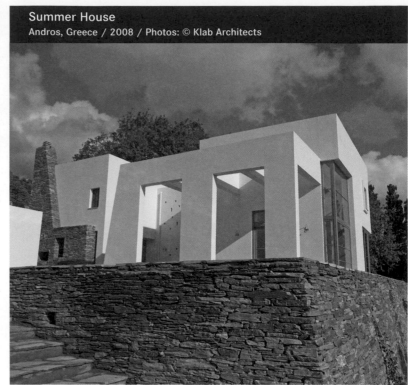

This country house on the island of Andros was built over the traditional platform or terrace which has been used to gain land for building from the uneven terrain of the islands dotting the Mediterranean.

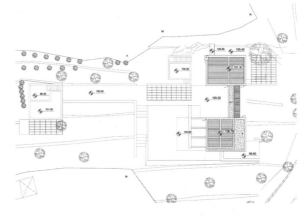

The predominance of white pays a kind of homage to traditional Greek architecture.

The commission called for the construction of a mixed-use complex that could change its functions depending on the season. The original idea led the architects to conceive a volume that was not too removed from the hilly landscape, which accounts for its low-rise design.

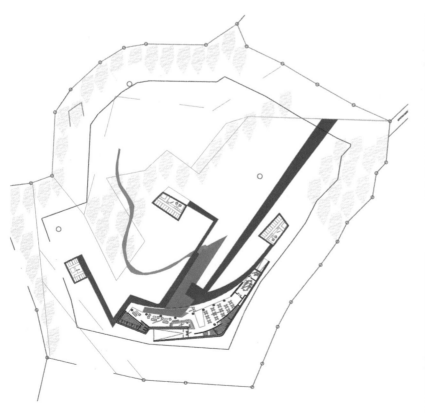

The main building has a floor space of 800 m² (8,611 sq ft), while the other buildings average 80 m² (861 sq ft).

The aim of this project was to offer its owners an oasis of peace in the middle of the city, which is achieved by means of a protective wall to isolate the interior space. The layout of the different rooms is influenced by this wall.

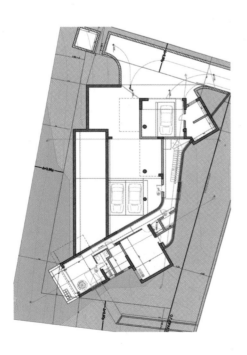

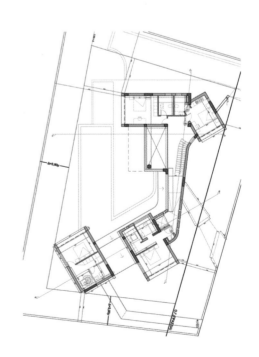

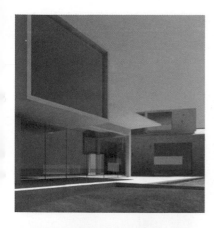

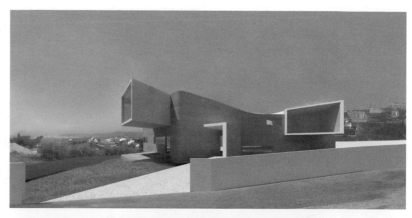

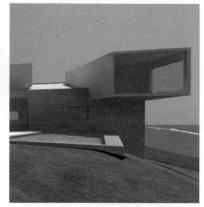

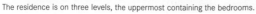
The residence is on three levels, the uppermost containing the bedrooms.

This project is a reinterpretation of the urban chaos that typifies the Greek capital, enabling the building to adapt to its setting. The design features a series of balcony-like cubicles.

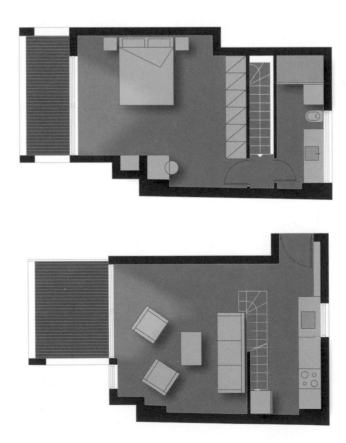

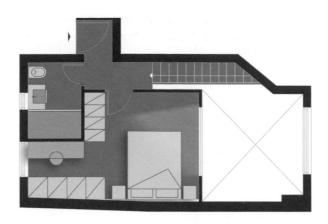

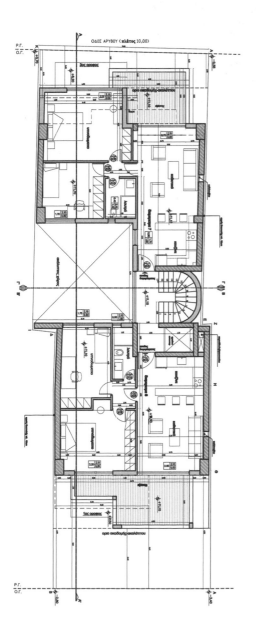

The project was adapted to a limited budget, which explains the simple finishes.

This house was designed to establish a dialogue between the two major architectural typologies present on the island—the hillside terraces and the traditional cube-shaped houses.

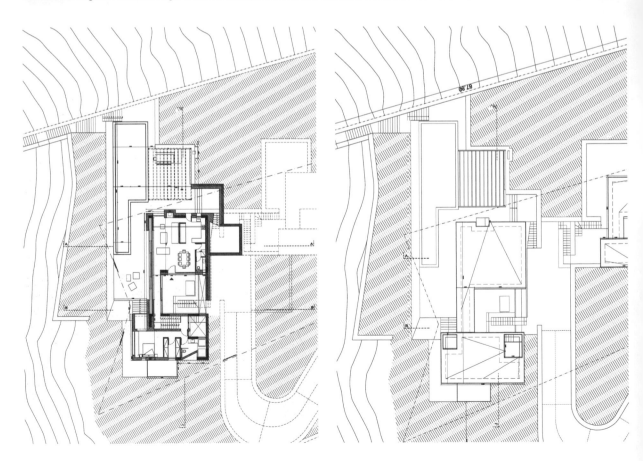

The stone retaining walls, *xerolithia*, were preserved as they stood on the site prior to the new building work.

Gemini

Herman Hertzberger

© Herman Hertzberger

Herman Hertzberger
Gerard Doustraat, 220
1073 XB Amsterdam, The Netherlands
Tel.: +31 20 676 58 88
www.hertzberger.nl

Herman Herztberger was born in Amsterdam in 1932 and graduated from the Technical University in Delft in 1958, the year he established his own architectural practice. He taught at the Academy of Architecture in Amsterdam between 1965 and 1969. Then from 1970 until 1999 he was a professor at the University he studied at. The most prestigious awards he has received include the Premio Vitruvio in 1998 for his entire career, the Golden Lion for the best foreign pavilion at the Venice Biennale in 2002, and the Richard Neutra Award in 1989.

## DWR Amsterdam

Amsterdam, The Netherlands / 2005 / Photos: © Duccio Malagamba

The new headquarters of the Amsterdam water and sewage management service consists of two towers bordering the Amstel River. The façades are given a spectacular appearance by a succession of windows forming a pattern resembling tiger stripes.

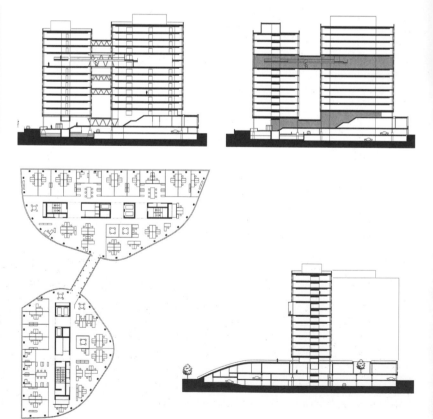

A series of four footbridges enable transit from one building to the other.

The angular form of the building is determined by the characteristics of the site, located at the end of a major avenue and opposite the Bonnefanten Museum. The façade is striking as a result of its diverse nature. Circular forms and right angles are abundantly featured.

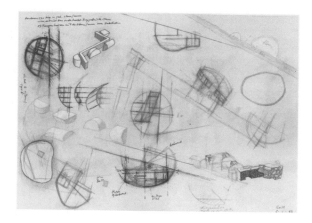

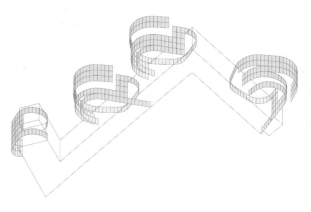

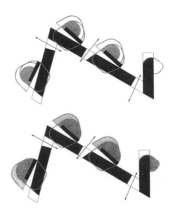

Cantilevered volumes are projected like large balconies and enable the different work spaces to be laid out efficiently.

## Fire Station
### Zwolle, The Netherlands / 2007 / Photos: © Jeroen Musch

The commission brief required the architect to provide the community with a "transparent" building. As a result, the interior is easily visible from the exterior. There is an open feel to the building and the visual focus is given to the different fire engines.

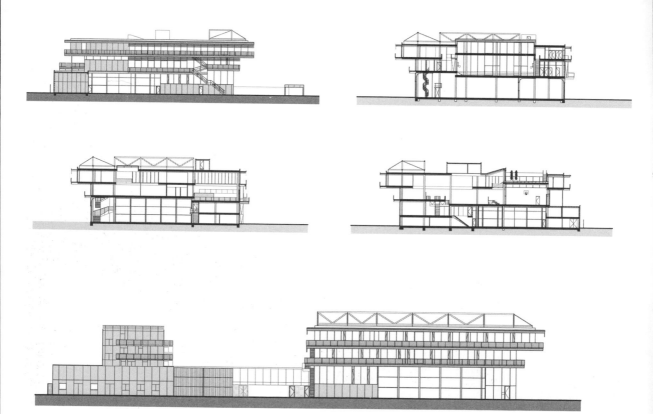

Another important requirement for the project was that vehicles and personnel could depart rapidly and simply in the shortest time possible.

The incredible transparency of the façade is the first thing that attracts attention to this office building. Not only can the layout of the interior be appreciated from the outside, but also the way the different levels are connected.

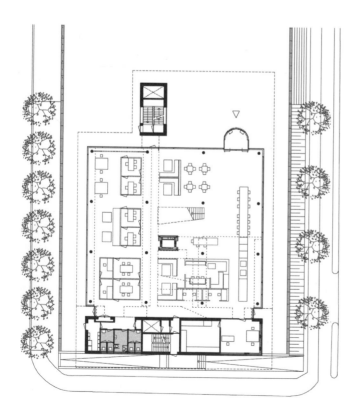

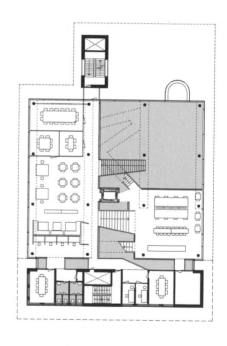

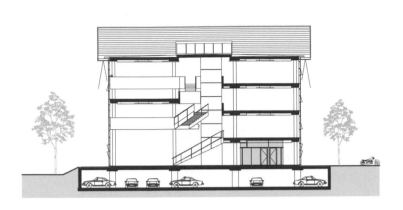

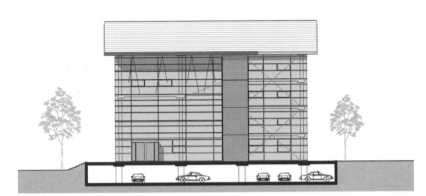

The interior features dramatic spaces created by the stairwell void.

This educational institution houses two elementary schools, a day care center, a playground, and a sports facility. The general design is based on the shape of the floor plan, giving the building length and dividing it into two very different parts.

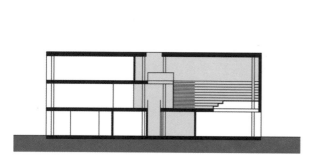

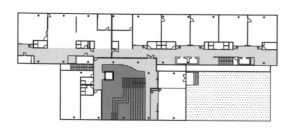

Entrances to the building are found at the north and south ends. These are connected by an internal street running the length of the site.

Hydra

## William Galloway & Koen Klinkers

### Dah-bee-deh House
Thailand / 2007 / Renderings: © Frontoffice

The main aim of this project was to design a building that would be as invisible as possible so as not to interrupt the visual continuity of the setting. To achieve this, the lower floor was given an open plan that reduces the weight of the structure.

Frontoffice
Mita Townhouse 4 B
Mita 2-chome 7-22, Minato-ku
Tokyo 108-0073, Japan
Tel.: +81 3 5484 3441
www.frontofficetokyo.com

William Galloway was born in Canada and studied architecture and environmental design at the University of Manitoba. He received a doctorate from the University of Tokyo in 2008. Before setting up Frontoffice, he worked for Fukumi Architects, Priestman Architects (London), and Jump Studios. Koen Klinkers was born in Herleen and studied architecture at the Technical University in Delft. Both architects set up Frontoffice in Tokyo in 2005, and in only three years have managed to make *Wallpaper*'s list of the 50 hottest new architecture practices.

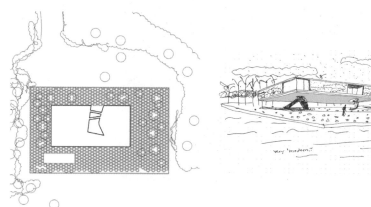

The stairs leading to the upper floor serve as structural pillars for the volume.

## Toyama Station

Toyama, Japan / To be determined / Renderings: © Frontoffice

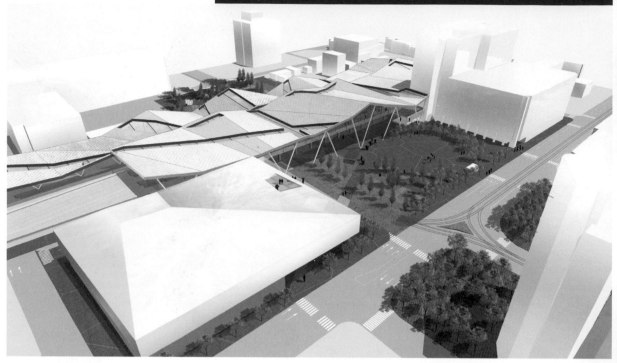

The design of this train station aims to make the infrastructure contained in it virtually invisible and to connect the north and south sides seamlessly without obstacles or partitions.

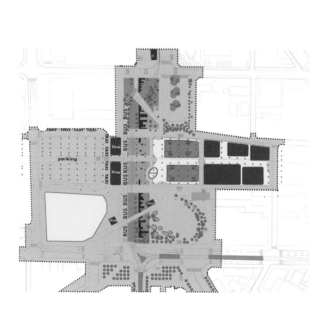

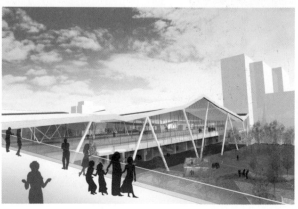

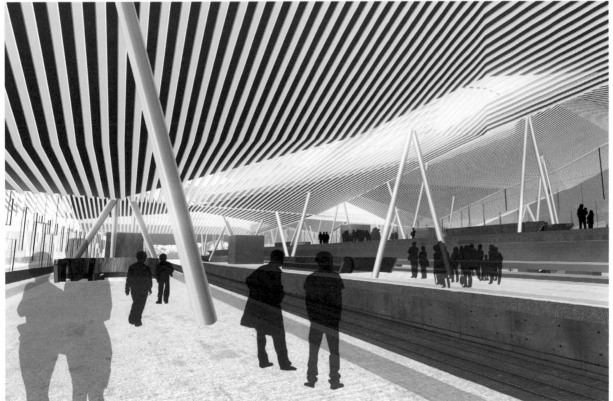

The visual focal point is the perforated roof, which mimics the nearby mountains.

Dorado

## Norman Foster

© Foster & Partners

Foster & Partners
Riverside, 22 Hester Road
SW11 4AN London, United Kingdom
Tel.: +44 20 7738 0455
www.fosterandpartners.com

Introductions are almost superfluous when speaking of Norman Foster. Born in Manchester, Foster graduated from the University of Manchester's School of Architecture before completing his studies at the Yale University. In 1967 he founded Foster & Partners, one of the firms responsible for the most outstanding projects in many disciplines that have been built in the world over the last 40 years. Awarded the Pritzker Prize in 1999 and the Praemium Imperiale in 2002, Foster has continued to take on major projects such as Beijing Airport and the Petronas University of Technology campus.

## Wembley Stadium

London, United Kingdom / 2007 / Photos: © Nigel Young, Foster & Partners

Designed as the first of a new generation of sports stadiums, the new Wembley stands out for the great variety of facilities it houses, including a large venue for events and a spacious waiting area for people attending functions.

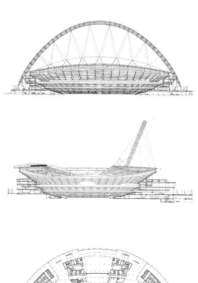

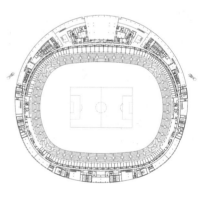

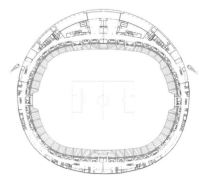

The most acclaimed feature is undeniably the partially retractable roof. It can close in one hour to provide shelter for up to 90,000 spectators.

## Dolder Grand Hotel

Zurich, Switzerland / 2006 / Photos: © Nigel Young, Foster & Partners

Majestically located on the shores of Lake Zurich, the remodeling project for this hotel called for its conversion into a luxury establishment. In order to achieve this, an extension was built that contrasts sharply with the earlier structure, and which has more than doubled the number of hotel rooms.

The new spaces contribute to the hotel being integrated with its natural surroundings.

## Hearst Tower
New York, NY, USA / 2006 / Photos: © Nigel Young, Foster & Partners

The new Hearst Tower is a volume that was added to the Art Deco building already existing on the site. The project aimed to give character to the building, leading to the dramatic silhouette of the new tower.

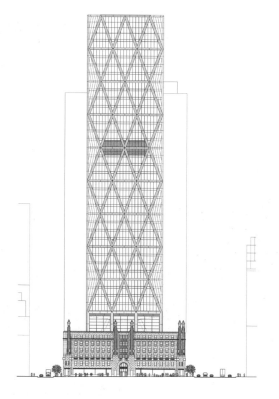

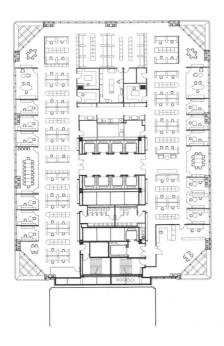

The new office spaces were designed to save a substantial amount of energy, and have become a role model for the intelligent office.

## Smithsonian Institution
Washington D. C., USA / 2007 / Photos: © Nigel Young, Foster & Partners

The design of this courtyard roof was created by means of 5,240 lines of computational coding. The roof consists of a steel frame painted white with a glass and aluminum cladding, together with a specially-designed fiber material for acoustic insulation of the space.

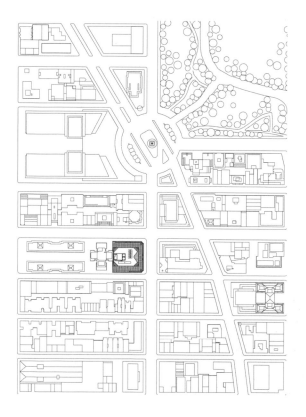

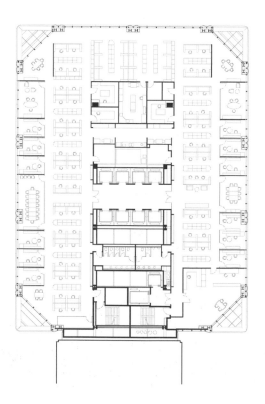

The columns are lined with anodized aluminum. The roof consists of a total of 864 panels, 92 of them triangular.

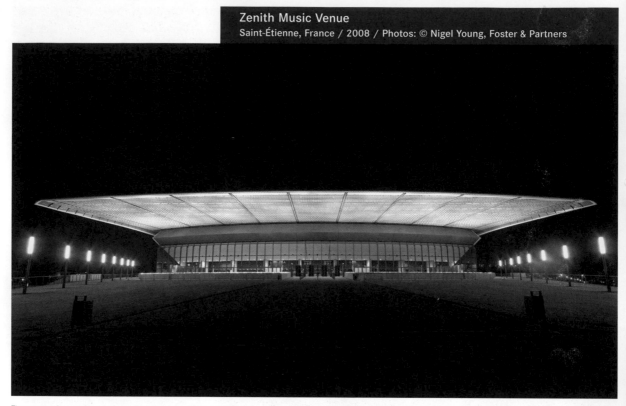

The spectacular aerodynamic form of this music and cultural venue is an architectural landmark. The cantilevered roof acts like a sail to channel air inside to ventilate and cool the interior.

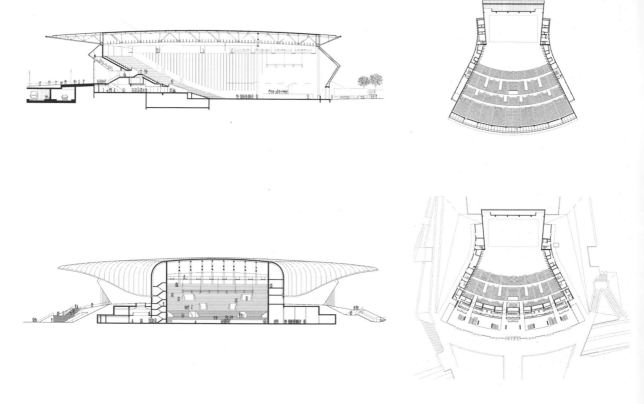

The auditorium can be configured to hold audiences of anywhere from 1,200 to 7,200 people.

Indus

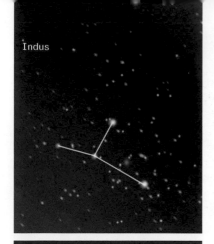

## Jorge Hernández de la Garza

© Jorge Hernández de la Garza

Jorge Hernández de la Garza
Álvaro Obregón, 278, int. 2.2
Col. Hipódromo Condesa
06100 Mexico City, Mexico
Tel.: +52 5 552 11 00 45
www.hernandezdelagarza.com

Born in Mexico in 1977, Jorge Hernández de la Garza studied at La Salle University in Mexico and won the Albert J. Pani Award in 1999. After several years working for the Abraham Zabludovsky studio and winning the Icons of Design Award for his project for the Vladimir Kaspé Cultural Center, among others, he established his own practice in 2007. He has participated in the Young Architects Annual Event and his works have been featured in publications in Japan, the United Kingdom, Spain, Brazil, and other countries.

## Invisible House
Mexico City, Mexico / 2010 / Renderings © Jorge Hernández de la Garza

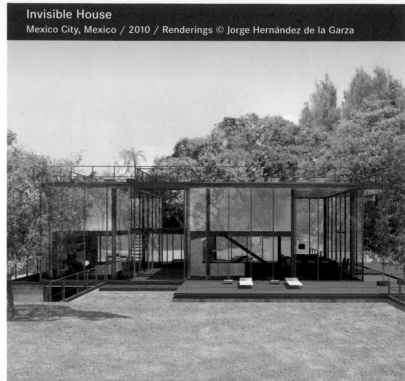

This striking glass box is located on a site filled with vegetation, turning the views into the focal point of the project. The façade is made up of vertically-positioned double glass panels measuring 5.2 × 1.25 m (17 × 4 ft).

The skeleton formed by steel beams and 10 columns is perfectly visible from the outside.

Located in the city of San Pedro Garza García, the challenge faced in this project was to design an office and home on the same site, making maximum use of the available land. To achieve this, it was necessary to create a mix of residential and office use over the four levels as permitted by zoning regulations.

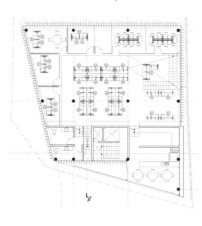

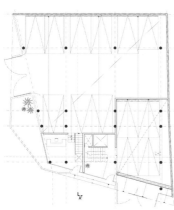

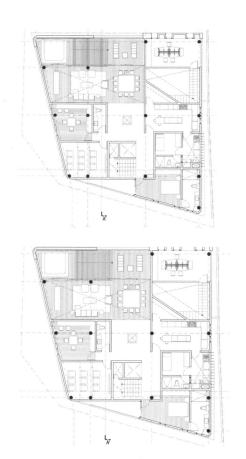

The uneven terrain influenced the dimensions of the building, which occupies 70 pecent of the site.

The double height of the living area and a thin folding glass skin blend the house into its setting and blur the line between interior and exterior.

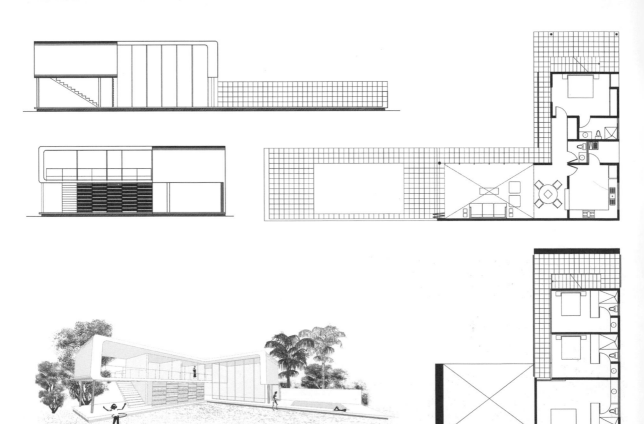

The residence will be located in a resort area of the state of Morelos, 60 km (37 miles) from the Mexican capital.

## Suntro House
### Oaxtepec, Mexico / 2006 / Photos: © Paul Czitrom

Located in a residential development with plentiful vegetation, the site faces towards the north east with incredible views of Mount Tepozteco and the best possible positioning to counteract the heat through natural ventilation.

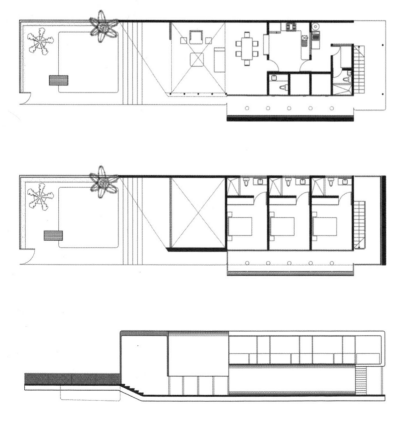

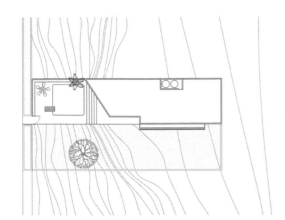

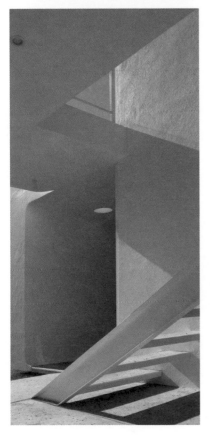

The exposed concrete floors provide a flowing feel, which also visually "cools" the interior.

Eridanus

Kazuyasu Kochi

Kochi Architect's Studio
302-1-36-21 Takada, Toshima-ku
Tokyo 171-0033, Japan
Tel.: +81 3 3986 0095
www.kkas.net

Kazuyasu Kochi was born in 1973 and graduated from the Tokyo National University of Fine Arts and Music in 2000. He then went to work at the Kazuhiko Namba & KAI studio. He established his own firm in 2003 and began teaching at the Shibaura Institute of Technology and the Kyoto Seika University in 2008. His main collaborators at Kochi Architect's Studio are Mana Kochi and Atsushi Motoyama.

## 4 Colors
Tokyo, Japan / 2006 / Photos: © Kazuyasu Kochi, Daici Ano

The raised location of this residence provides fabulous views and long hours of sunlight, which is uncommon in a city as congested as Tokyo. Each level is a single room lined in materials of different colors.

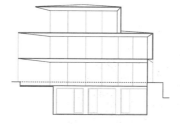

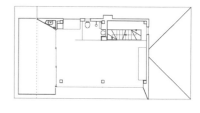

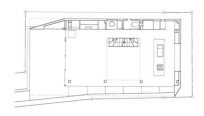

Each level has a closet, bathroom, and storage rooms on the north and west walls.

## House KN

Kanagawa, Japan / 2006 / Photos: © Nobumitsu Watanabe, Kazuysu Kochi

The design of this suburban residence is based on an imaginary box placed over the available site. A large void was then cut out to form a window, opening the habitable area out to the small garden.

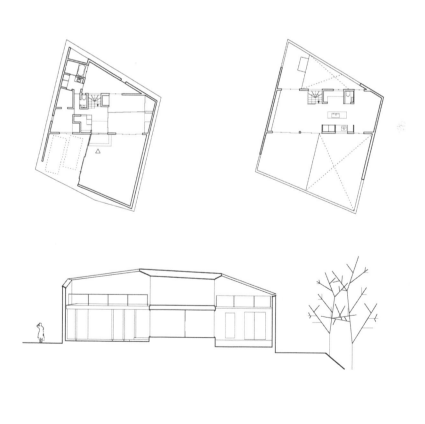

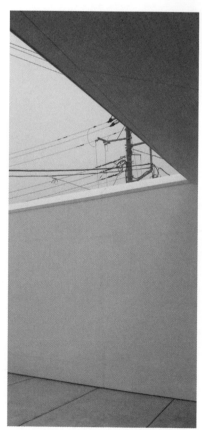

The slope of the outer wall is designed to offer the best views possible.

The owner of this residence commissioned a project that would enable good views of the surrounding rice fields to be enjoyed from the roof. This led to the inclined shape of the volume, which rises as a kind of visual diving board.

The extremely simple construction made use of prefabricated and assembled wooden panels.

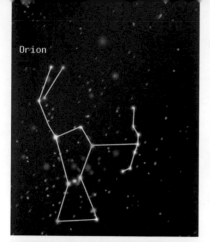

## Vinko Penezić & Krešimir Rogina

© Penezić & Rogina

Penezić & Rogina Architects
Antuna Bauera, 8
10000 Zagreb, Croatia
Tel.: +385 1 390 6331
www.penezic-rogina.com

Vinko Penezić, born in Zagreb, Croatia, in 1959, and Krešimir Rogina, born in Rijeka, Croatia, in 1959, have been working together since 1979. Both are alumni of the Zagreb School of Architecture. They took postgraduate studies at the University of Belgrade and founded a joint practice in 1991. Their projects have been particularly successful in Japan, where they have won six design competitions. They have taken part in the Venice Biennale on a number of occasions and have received such acknoledgements as the 2002 Vladimir Nazor Award and the 1997 Bernardo Bernardi Award.

## Jarun Kindergarten
Zagreb, Croatia / 2006 / Photos: © Damil Kalogjera

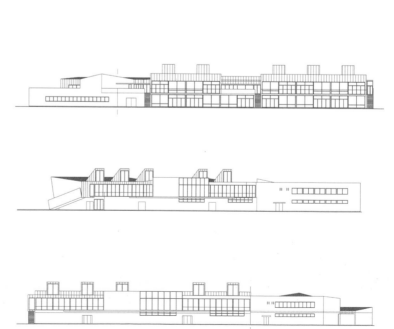

This school is comprised of three interconnected spaces: a daycare center on the lower level, a kindergarten on both lower and upper levels, and administration areas bordering the garden on the west side.

Synthetic wall cladding in bright colors creates an appealing atmosphere for children attending the school.

Containing two courts, service areas and commercial premises, this complex also features a VIP area, press center and club and federation offices.

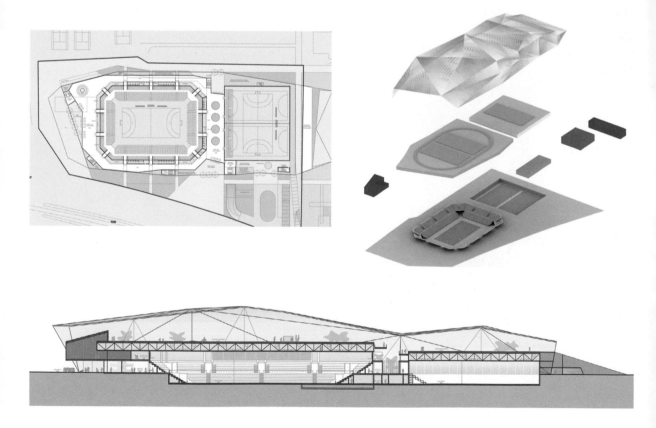

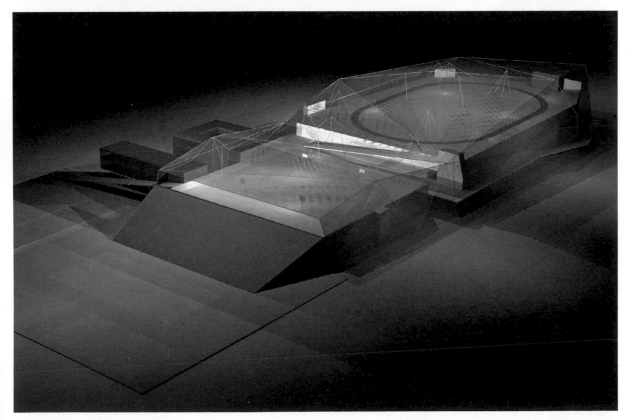

The main stadium holds around 5,000 spectators.

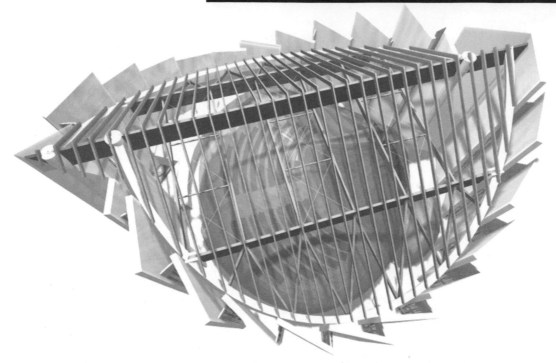

This radical remodeling of this spiritual center responds to the need to remove certain elements from the building that take away from the atmosphere of retreat expected of a space like this. The key feature of the project is the installation of a translucent polycarbonate membrane separate from the earlier structure.

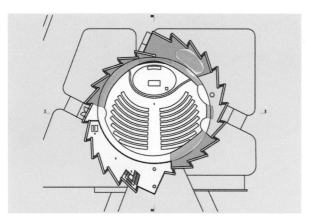

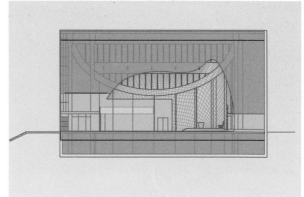

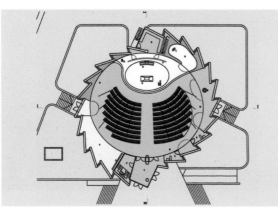

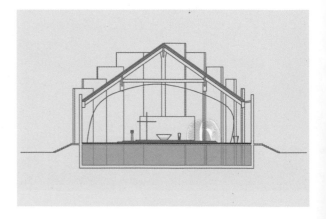

The new membrane enloses the previously disperse spaces and creates a more secluded atmosphere.

Mensa

## Kees Christiaanse

KCAP Architects & Planners
Piekstraat, 27
3071 EL Rotterdam, The Netherlands
Tel.: +31 10 789 03 00
www.kcap.eu

Born in Amsterdam in 1953, Kees Christiaanse studied at the University of Delft and graduated in 1988. His degree project, Kavel 25, won him the Berlage Award. In 1989 he established his own firm in Rotterdam. He was a professor of architecture and urban planning at the Technical University of Berlin, and currently teaches in institutes in Switzerland and London. In 2009 he was the curator of the Rotterdam International Architecture Biennale.

## Wijnhaven Island
### Rotterdam, The Netherlands / 2009 / Photos: © KCAP

Located on an island strategically located between the city of Rotterdam and the Maas River, this complex shows its awareness of the future urban development of the remaining lots occupying the site.

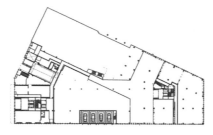

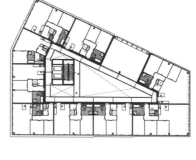

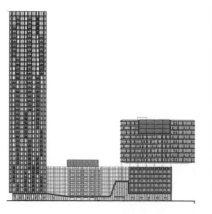

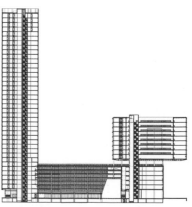

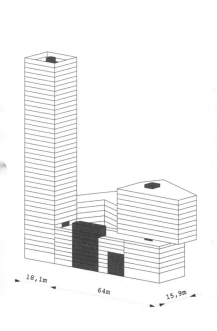

18,1m  64m  15,9m

The volumes are dominated by a rectangular glass box suspended over a sparse succession of columns that give the complex a monumental character.

Having received a commission for an office building adapted to the needs of different types of companies, the architect designed an "omnidirectional" structure, with rounded forms and a copper-clad façade.

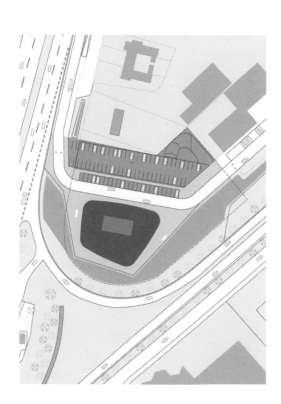

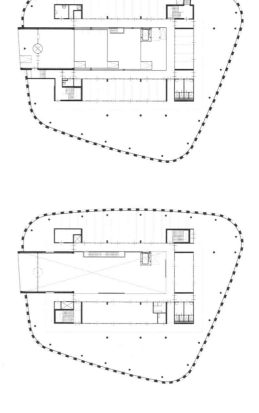

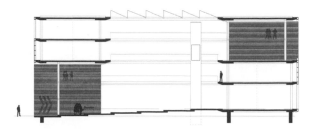

The façade displays a pattern that gives a feeling of rhythm, with large windows.

This pair of towers measuring 86 and 70 m (282 and 230 ft) in height, respectively, will be the first energy-neutral office complex in The Netherlands. This means the buildings will produce as much clean energy as they consume, so their $CO_2$ emissions will amount to zero.

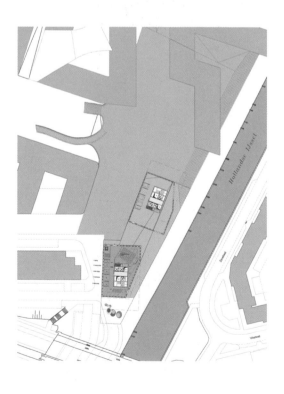

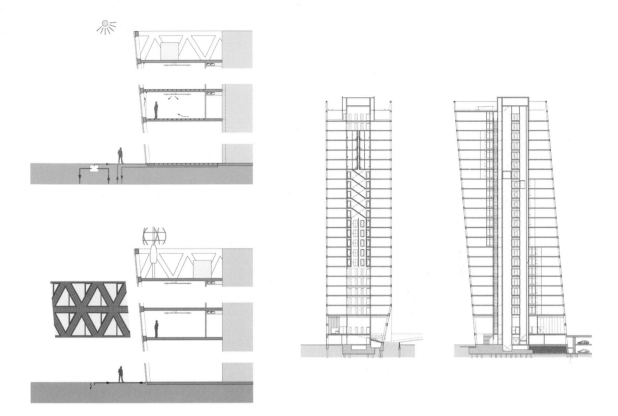

The tallest tower will have wind turbines and a biofuel generator on the roof.

The new Eindhoven airport terminal was built next to the old one, between the access road and the runway. It is a light and transparent structure comprising three areas—a foyer, passenger service space, and an upper level with offices and shops.

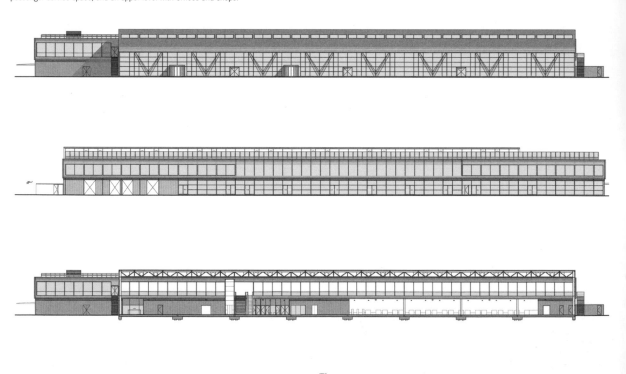

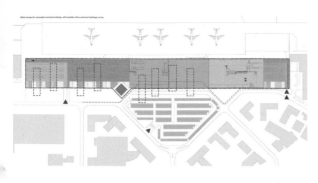

The aerodynamic form of the façade is a tribute to aeronautics.

## East Office Building

Hamburg, Germany / 2003 / Photos: © H. G. Esch

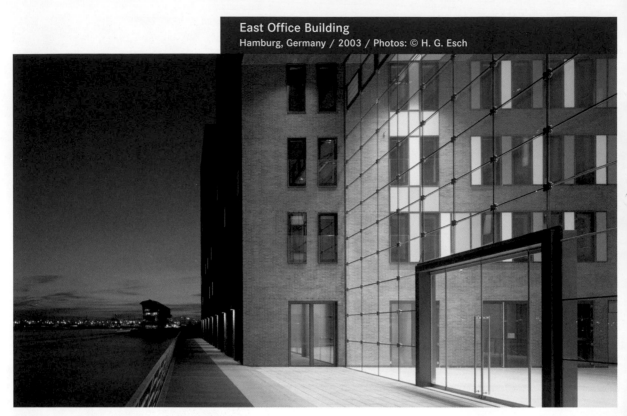

This project belongs to a complex comprising three large office buildings and giving a monumental aspect to the new business area on the Hamburg waterfront. The construction of an adjoining high-rise residential tower called "Kristall" has been planned.

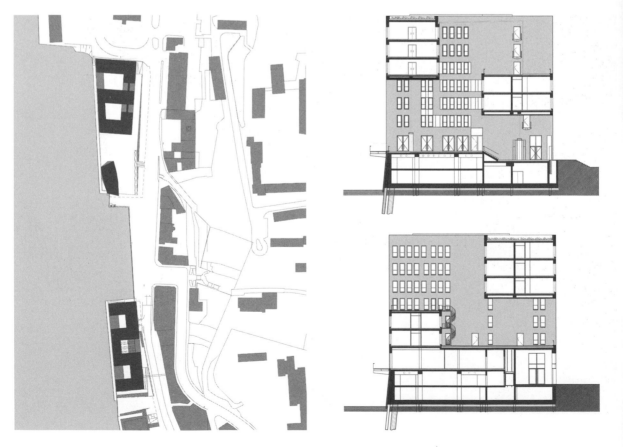

All of the buildings in the complex have the same design of a deep, glassed inner courtyard.

Located in an old dock area currently being converted into a residential district, this complex of totally different buildings aims to lend character to the new urban setting. The contrast of brick and glass façades appears to connect the past with the present.

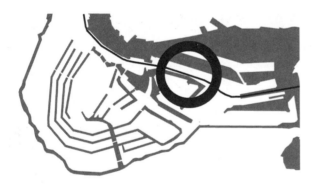

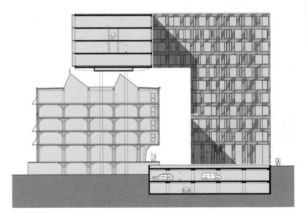

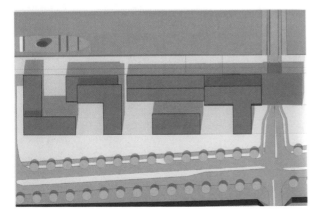

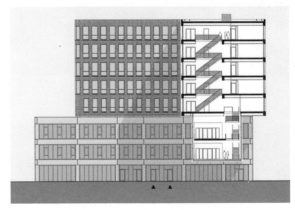

Aside from supervising the entire project, KCAP Architects & Planners also designed the parking garages and was responsible for the general technical coordination.

Norma

## Klaus Mayer & Petra Sattler-Smith

© Kevin G. Smith

Mayer Sattler-Smith
1104 West 7th Avenue
Anchorage, AK 99501, USA
Tel.: +1 907 277 7878
www.mayersattler-smith.com

Klaus Mayer studied at the University of Stuttgart and has lived in Alaska since 1995. In 1999 he was elected president of the Alaska Design Forum and was named a Loeb fellow by the Harvard University Design School for the 2004-2005 academic year. A graduate of the Darmstadt University of Technology, Petra Sattler-Smith arrived in Alaska in 1996. Five years later she founded her practice with Mayer as a partner. In 2004 they received an AIA Alaska honor award for their design of the Kotlik K-12 school.

## 13th and a Street
Anchorage, AK, USA / 2006 / Photos: © Kevin G. Smith

This project consists of six horizontally laid-out residential units with views of the Chugach Mountains and the Anchorage skyline. Each unit has an outdoor space and an open-plan lower level.

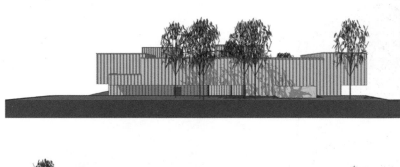

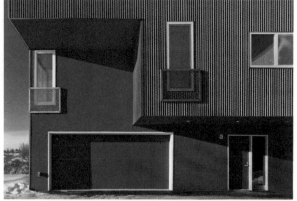

Features include radiant floor heating, a free-floating fireplace, and a skylight in the master bedroom.

## Ideal House
### Anchorage, AK, USA / 2007 / Photos: © Kevin G. Smith

Divided into modules that mark the limits of the different spaces, this house also features a multi-functional space: the garage, which also serves as a storeroom. In addition to providing a parking space for the car, it provides orderly storage space for bicycles and the lawn mower.

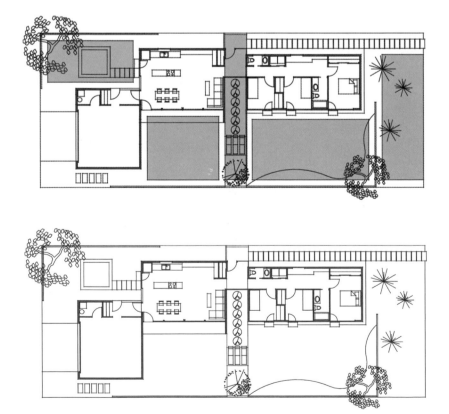

Wood is the predominant feature of the façade and also has an important presence inside the house.

Laid out from east to west, the long plan of this residence was designed to maximize solar exposure. The lower level contains all of the private areas, while the upper level is for common living areas.

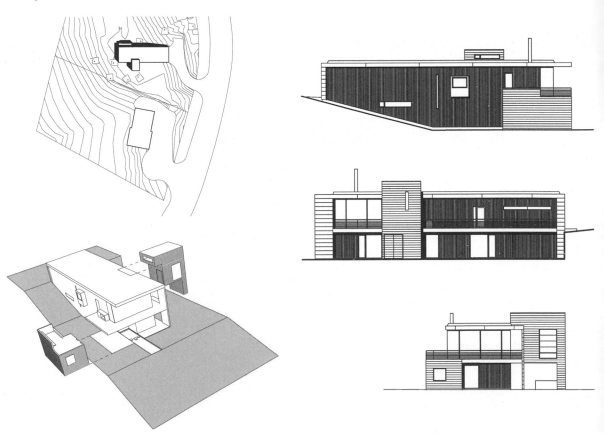

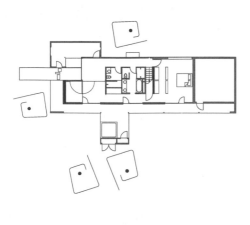

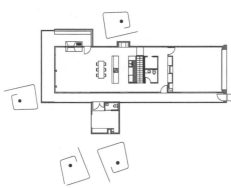

It was important to open up some of the façades to the magnificent views of the surrounding areas, as seen through the living area window.

Aries

## Paul de Ruiter

Architentenbureau Paul de Ruiter
Leidsestraat, 8-10
1017 XB Amsterdam, The Netherlands
Tel.: +31 20 626 32 44
www.paulderuiter.nl

Paul de Ruiter, born in 1962, graduated with honor from the Delft University of Technology. In 1994 he founded Architectenbureau Paul de Ruiter, a firm that is particularly concerned with designing settings that facilitate coexistence and the full integration of buildings in their surrounding landscape. A member of the Living Daylights Foundation and a professor at different universities of technology in his country, Paul de Ruiter routinely collaborates with specialist media and is devoted to the establishment of a more sustainable society through collaborations with different institutions.

## Rijkswaterstaat Zeeland
Middelburg, The Netherlands / 2004 / Photos: © Rob 't Hart, Pieter Kers

The presence of sunlight is very important in this office building. The south façade is 50 percent glass, while this proportion rises to 100 percent on the north façade. The canopy-like skylights installed on the outer layers enable light to enter the entire building at a greater angle.

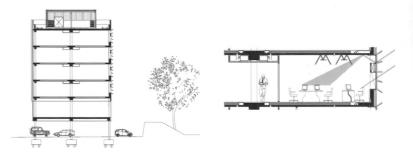

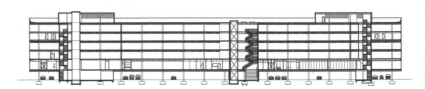

The flexible construction of the new Rijkswaterstaat Zeeland offices offers the possibility for the building to be divided in different ways, depending on needs that may arise for the company.

Zoning laws determined the dimensions and height of this parking garage designed over nine levels: four underground levels, four above-ground levels and a commercial floor at street level. The floor plan is a trapezoid with rounded corners, providing smooth transit.

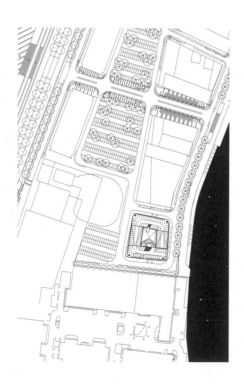

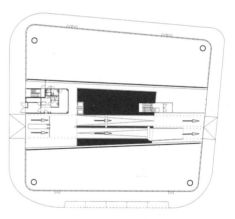

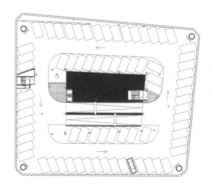

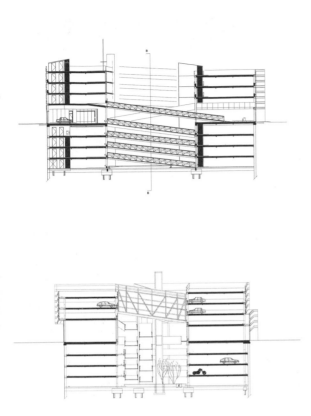

The perforated aluminum panels on the façade filter sunlight and also turn the building into a source of artificial illumination at night.

The main inspiration for this residence was its location on the shore of a lake. This determined the outward facing design and the installation of floor-to-ceiling windows to take greatest advantage of the views. The result is that the volume almost appears to be a floating wooden box, transparent at times.

The glass façade runs almost seamlessly around the living spaces, with an effect of almost complete transparency.

This multi-purpose building contains spaces for a theater, a theater school, and a circus. Located next to a lake, the building has an elliptical shape and features a façade illuminated with energy-saving LED lighting systems.

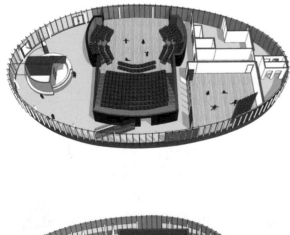

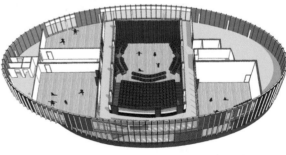

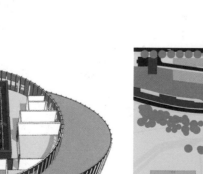

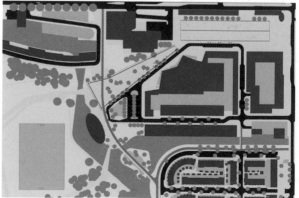

With ceilings reaching almost 7 m (23 ft) to house all kinds of shows, and with a capacity to seat 220 people, the interior was designed for an impressive variety of uses.

Chamaeleon

## Hitoshi Abe

© Atelier Hitoshi Abe

### FRP
Sendai, Japan / 2007 / Photos: © Daici Ano

This apartment building is designed like a tree where each level is accessed independently by means of an elevator taken on the second floor. The overlapping of levels on planes is a feature of the exterior.

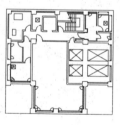

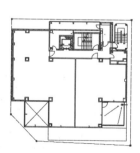

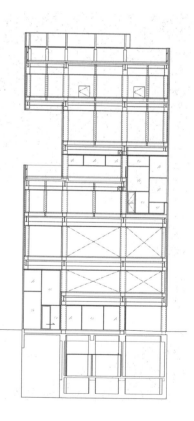

Atelier Hitoshi Abe
3-3-16 Oroshimachi, Wakabayashi-ku
Sendai, Miyagi 984-0015, Japan
Tel.: +81 2 2284 3411
www.a-slash.jp

Born in Sendai in 1962, Hitoshi Abe studied in California and worked for the Coop Himmelb(l)au between 1988 and 1992, the year he set up his own practice. Professor at both the Institute of Technology and the University of Tohoku during the 1990s, he also taught at UC Berkeley and UCLA. Outstanding among the acknowledgments he has received are the Good Design Award for a factory in Sasaki, the International Architecture Award for the Kanno Museum project, and the Tohoku Architectural Award for the Michinoku Folklore Museum.

The window frames are placed at differing heights, as are the prefabricated panels on the façade.

This building houses a pediatric clinic run by a couple living on the upper levels. The third level of the building seems to float above the lower ones, and is supported by eight steel columns that create an open space.

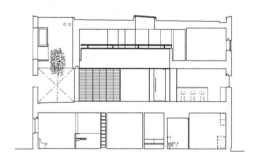

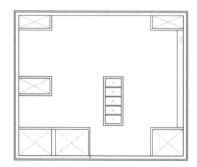

The common areas of the home occupy the second level, which is more open plan.

'Columba'

## Farshid Moussavi & Alejandro Zaera-Polo

© Valerie Bennet

Foreign Office Architects
55 Curtain Road
EC2A 3PT London, United Kingdom
Tel.: +44 20 7033 9800
www.f-o-a.net

Farshid Moussavi and Alejandro Zaera-Polo founded Foreign Office Architects in 1995. Almost right from the start the relevance of their projects raised them to a privileged position among the most prestigious architectural firms in Europe. Their most well-known projects include the Spanish Pavilion at the Aichi Expo and the Yokohama International Port Terminal, to name but a few. Representing the United Kingdom at the 2002 International Architecture Exhibition at the Venice Biennale, the firm has received three RIBA awards, the Enric Miralles Prize, and the Charles Jencks Award.

## International Port Terminal
Yokohama, Japan / 2002 / Photos: © Satoru Mishima

This port terminal has been sculptured with spectacular relief and has become an architectural landmark in the area. An attractive wooden roof hides practically the entire workings of the center.

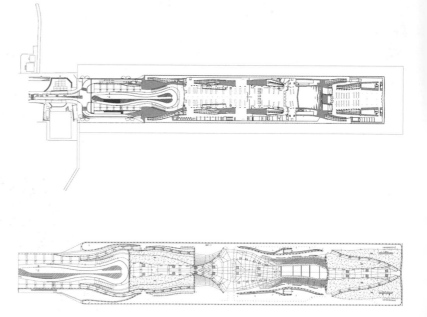

The parking garage is striking for its space and its location inside the "whale belly" that gives the project its form.

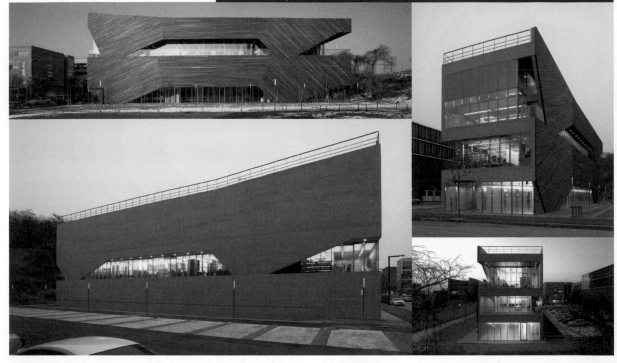

## Dulnyouk Publishers
Seoul, South Korea / 2005 / Photos: © Kim Jae-Kyung

This modern office building occupies a 2,000 m² (21,530 sq ft) site on the edge of a hill. The main façade displays two boat-shaped trapezoidal structures, while the sides illuminate the exterior through expanses of glass.

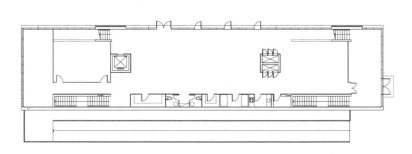

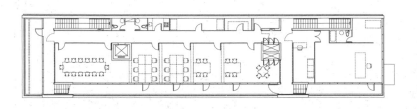

406

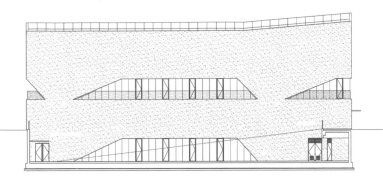

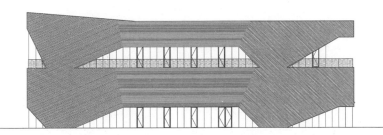

The complex contains office space, storage space, an event space, and an apartment for guests.

A simple limestone façade with few openings is the distinguishing feature of this apparently monolithic and somber building. The 650-seat theater makes full use of a limited site in the center of this resort town.

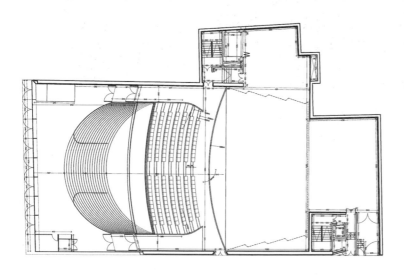

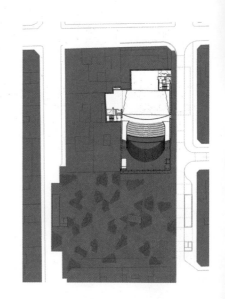

As it gains height, the interior floor plan expands to provide more space.

This complex of 100 social housing units on the outskirts of Madrid was a challenge for the firm, which had to design the project on a limited budget. The eye-catching pattern created by the vertical screens on the façade is clearly the most distinguishing feature of the project.

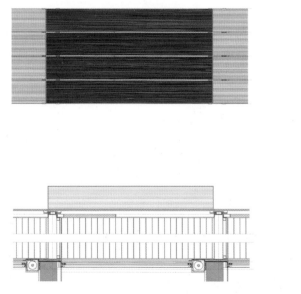

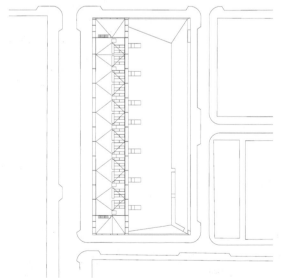

The contemporary feel of the succession of vertical rectangles formed by the windows stand out over any of the project's other architectural solutions.

This IT research center is located in a beautiful setting beside the Iregua River. This position inspired the architects to integrate the volume into the natural surroundings, resulting in partially external passageways and its semi-sunken feel.

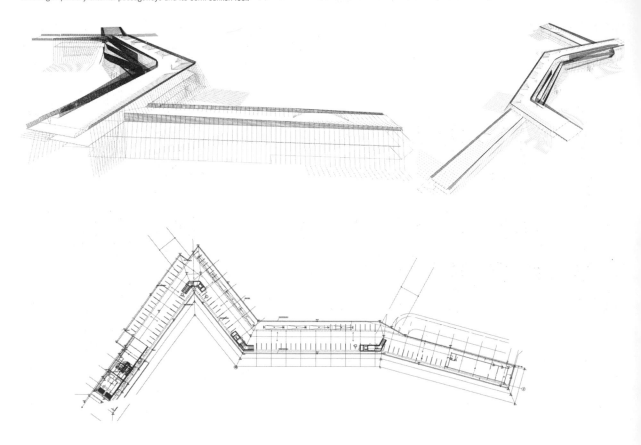

Made from diagonal steel cables, an exoskeleton that barely creates a barrier separates the transit areas from the garden. This screen will be covered with vines in the future.

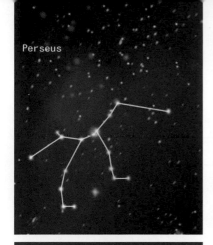

Perseus

## Uwe R. Brückner

© Frieder Daubenberger

Atelier Brückner GmbH
Krefelder Straße, 32
70376 Stuttgart, Germany
Tel.: +49 71 15 00 07 70
www.atelier-brueckner.de

The philosophy of Atelier Brückner is focused on creating spaces around a concept. They consider architecture as a kind of scenography. With over 60 collaborators working on their projects, the team has won countless Red Dot Awards and iF Awards, and stage design is an important part of their work.

## BMW Museum
Munich, Germany / 2007 / Photos: © Marcus Meyer

Although the BMW project already features in the pages of this book, the museum in the same complex, the work of Atelier Brückner, deserves a mention of its own. The structure is inspired by the world of automobiles, particularly in the shape of four cylinders and the BMW marque. The result is dynamism as architecture.

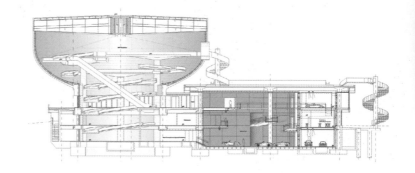

The main idea behind the interiors was to create the feeling that the street continues under the roof.

This is the first museum in China dedicated exclusively to the automobile. A line marks out a route through the permanent collection. Each exhibited piece is inserted into a specific space, so that the different cars can create a strong visual impact.

As visitors pass through the different spaces, they have the sensation of being on a journey.

Bearing in mind that the theme of the event was the responsible use of water and sustainable development, the architects accepted the challenge of designing the Pavilion of the African Countries guided by a clear premise: the intelligent use of materials.

The façades of the Pavilion of the African Countries evoke the forms of that continent's characteristic landscape.

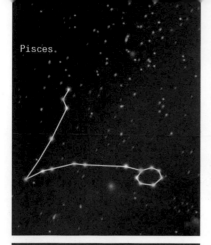

Pisces.

## Jean Nouvel

Ateliers Jean Nouvel
10, Cité d'Angoulême
75001 Paris, France
Tel.: +33 1 49 23 83 83
www.jeannouvel.com

Jean Nouvel was born in Fumel, France, in 1945. In 1976 he became one of the co-founders of the Mars 1976 architectural movement. Responsible for his own projects since 1970, he received the silver medal from the French Academy of Architecture in 1983. He founded Ateliers Jean Nouvel in 1994, and in 2001 received the Royal Gold Medal of the Royal Institute of British Architects. His entire career was acknowledged when he won the 2008 Pritzker Prize.

## Philharmonie de Paris
Paris, France / 2012 / Renderings: © Ateliers Jean Nouvel

Located in Parc de la Villette, this striking 2,400-seat concert hall will have floor space of 2,000 m² (21,530 sq ft). The project has a budget of 286 million dollars (200 million euros).

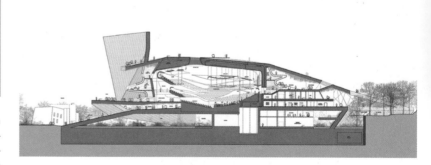

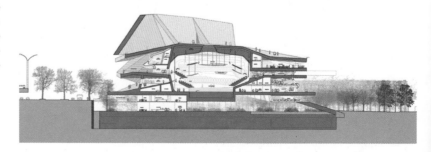

The free-form façade and large interior spaces are striking features of the design.

Located on a block bounded by Mercer and Grand Streets and Broadway, this residential building was initially designed as a hotel, but the project was changed in the wake of the events of 9/11. However, the exterior aspect was kept, owing to its design fitting in appropriately with its surroundings.

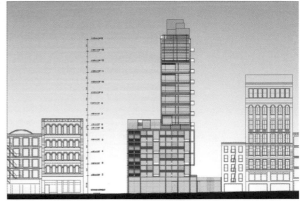

Inside are at least 10 different layouts, ranging from two-room apartments to a duplex of over 300 m² (3,230 sq ft).

Extending over a total of 24,000 m² (260,000 sq ft) and at a cost of 143 million dollars (100 million euros), this museum will have the appearance of a dome structure that appears to be floating.

The permanent collection will take up 6,000 m² (64,600 sq ft), while temporary exhibitions will have an area of about 2,000 m² (21,530 sq ft).

Located in an emerging neighborhood, the architect established a landmark for the surrounding urban context with the solid volume he designed for this concert hall. Seen from the outside, the simplicity of forms gives it a certain monumental character.

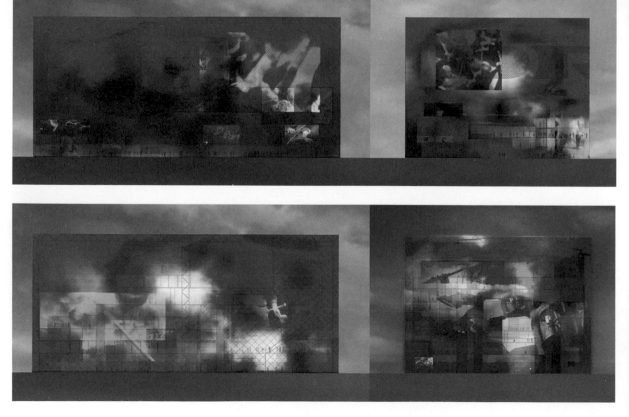

The interiors have a more complex design, with importance given to differentiating the various spaces.

## Agbar Tower
Barcelona, Spain / 2005 / Photos: © Philippe Ruault

Barcelona's water management company commissioned Jean Nouvel to design a tower for its headquarters that would also be an architectural landmark to change the city's skyline. Thousand of small glass panes at varying angles of inclination form the façade.

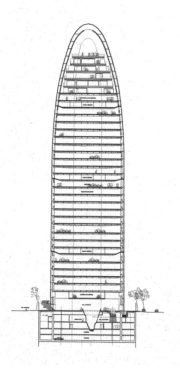

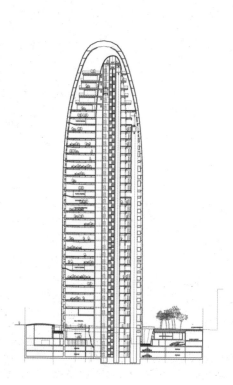

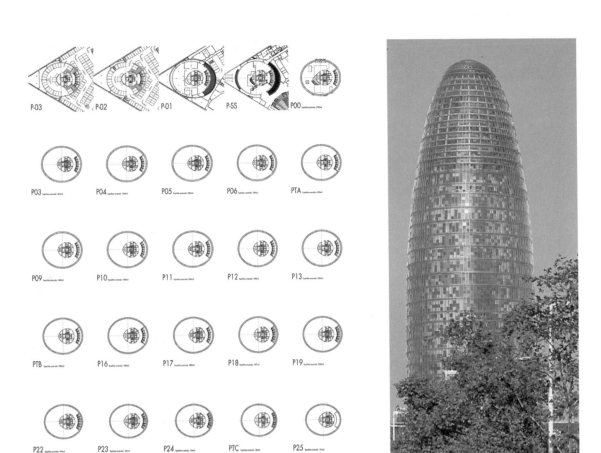

The floors comprise the sum of spaces around the communications core containing the stairs and elevators.

The 1,700 glass rectangles of different sizes are the most striking feature of this project located in New York's Chelsea district. The transparent façade is in keeping with the privileged location of the building.

The floors contain a total of 72 luxury apartments.

Corona Borealis

## Francine Houben

© Mecanoo Architecten

Mecanoo Architecten
Ode Delft, 203
2611 HD Delft, The Netherlands
Tel.: +31 15 279 81 00
www.mecanoo.com

"May it also be beautiful?" This question by Antoine de Saint-Exupéry has served the Dutch firm as slogan and leitmotif during its 20-year history. Founded in the 1980s by Francine Houben, Mecanoo is a multi-disciplinary practice that has always stressed the aesthetic finish of its projects and which, over the years, has received acknowledgments such as the 2009 International Design Award for FiftyTwoDegrees, the 2007 Brick Award, and the 2007/2008 Dedalo Mionosse Award for Sustainability. Professor at the Technical University in Delft, Francine Houben directed the Rotterdam International Architecture Biennale in 2003.

## Center for the Performing Arts
Taiwan / To be determined / Renderings: © Mecanoo Architecten

Seating 5,800 spectators, this new cultural complex takes its inspiration from the banyan tree, which spread so much that, according to legend, Alexander the Great was able to shelter his entire army inside one.

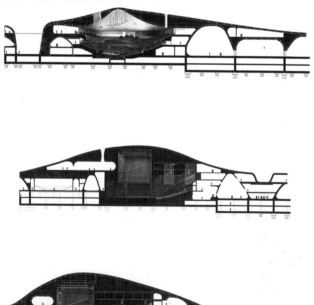

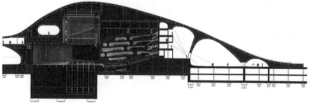

With a surface area of 115,000 m² (1,237,850 sq ft), this complex is one of the most important projects undertaken by the firm to date.

This spectacular building is set on the banks of the Segre River and rises like a great geode in all of its stony splendor. A wide ramp leads to the foyer, where panoramic views will be had from the second level through a large expanse of glass.

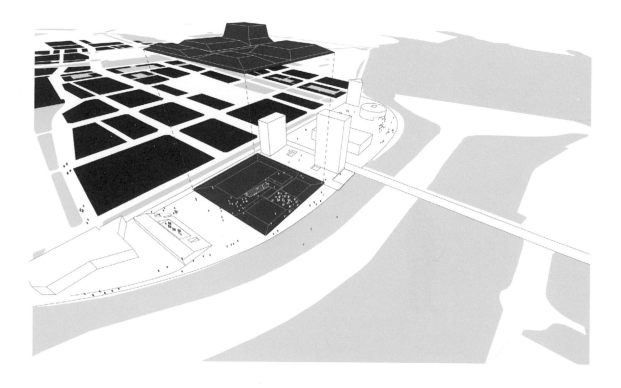

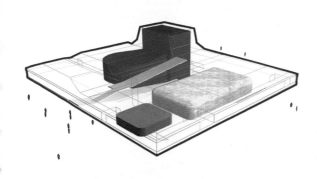

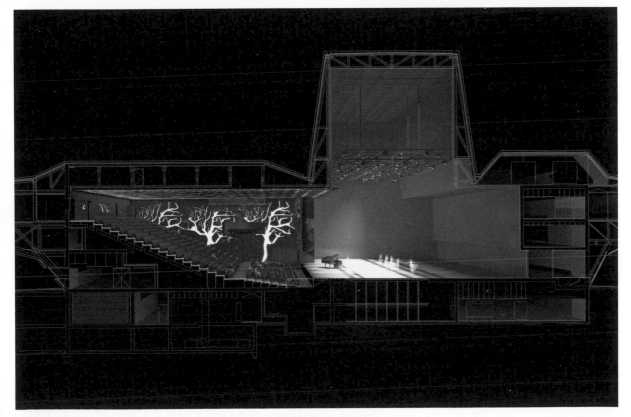

Also part of the plan is the construction of a garden on the central roof, which will serve as a vantage point.

Puppis

## Dietmar Feichtinger

© Dietmar Feichtinger Architectes

**Dietmar Feichtinger Architectes**
11, rue des Vignoles
75020 Paris, France
Tel.: +33 1 43 71 15 22
www.feichtingerarchitectes.com

Dietmar Feichtinger studied architecture at the University of Graz. Between 1984 and 1988 he worked in the same institution with Professors Giencke and Kada. He spent the next four years in the firm of Philippe Chaix and Jean-Paul Morel before founding his own practice. He has taught at the University of Innsbruck and at the Paris la Villette University. Dietmar Feichtinger opened an office in Vienna in 2002.

## University
### Krems, Austria / 2005 / Photos: © Barbara Feichtinger

The new building for the University of Applied Sciences in Krems is an example of "transparent architecture," largely promoted by many of Dietmar Feichtinger's works. The design of the glass, steel and aluminum façade contrasts with neighboring buildings and creates a true architectural landmark on the university campus of this Austrian town.

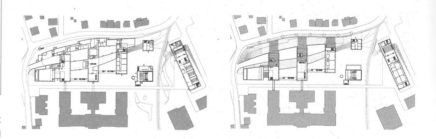

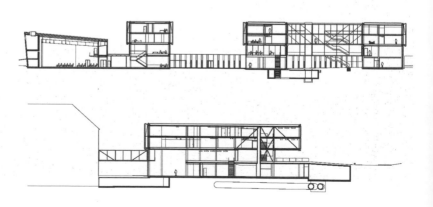

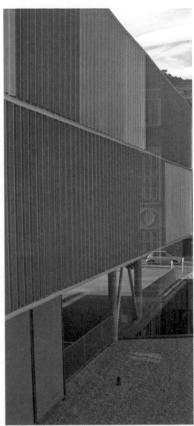

Discreet pillars make these three impressively large translucent modules appear to float in the air.

With a total length of 304 m (1,000 ft), of which 190 m (625 ft) are a free span, this striking footbridge connects Bercy Park with the François Mitterand National Library, a crossing that was previously only possible by boat across the Seine.

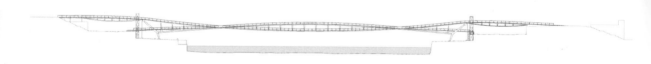

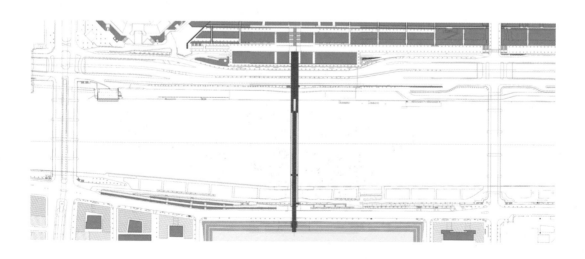

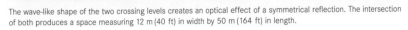

The wave-like shape of the two crossing levels creates an optical effect of a symmetrical reflection. The intersection of both produces a space measuring 12 m (40 ft) in width by 50 m (164 ft) in length.

With a budget of over 43 million dollars (30 million euros) and a total surface area of 40,000 m² (430,560 sq ft), this huge complex combines very different architectural typologies, all with the common denominator of a translucent façade.

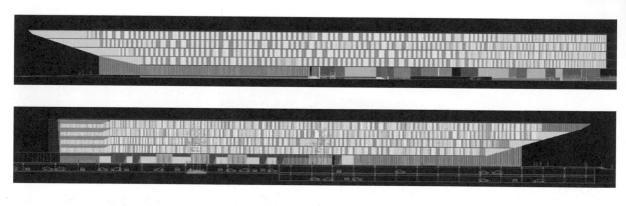

The curved forms of the volumes are another unifying feature of the project.

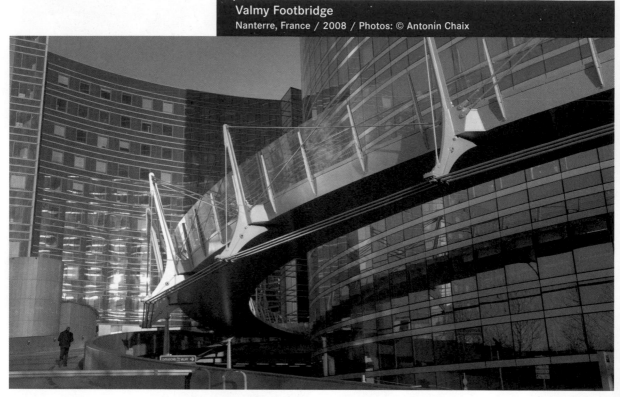

## Valmy Footbridge
Nanterre, France / 2008 / Photos: © Antonin Chaix

This footbridge winds 90 m (295 ft) through the dense urban fabric of the business district of La Défense. A series of "vertebrae" and "tendons" maintains the rigidity of the structure.

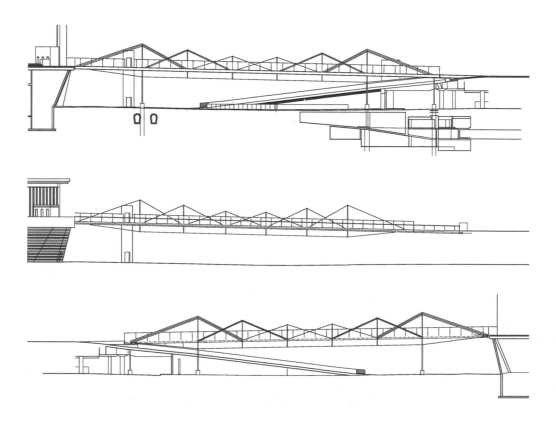

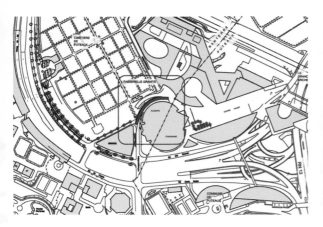

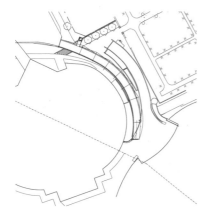

A series of glass panes form the railing and enable the surrounding cityscape to be contemplated.

Seemingly floating without supports, the most striking thing about this building is the amazing lightness with which the levels are stacked and the spaces are laid out without the building gaining too much height.

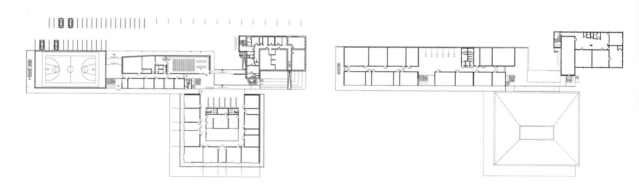

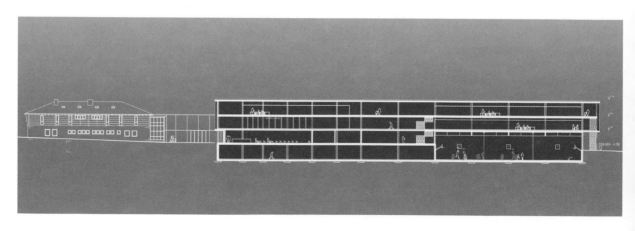

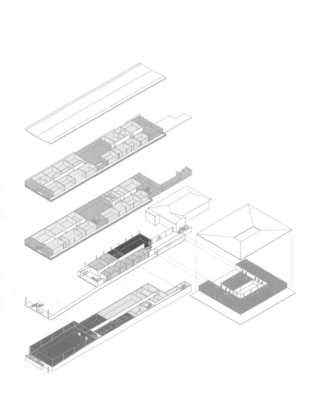

The complex extends over a total surface area of 11,000 m² (118,500 sq ft).

This complex located in Weiz divides its surface area into 2,440 m² (26,000 sq ft) of cultural space—including a 645-seat auditorium, 2,870 m² (31,000 sq ft) of parking and 1,840 m² (20,000 sq ft) of offices and commercial premises.

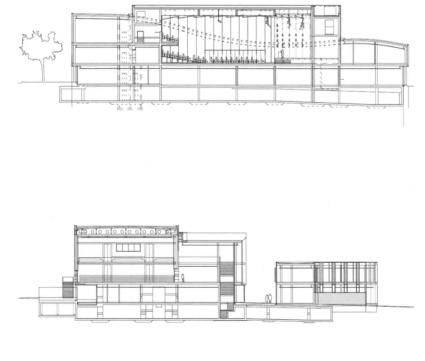

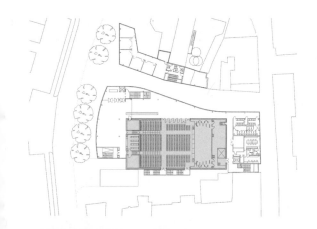

The curved glass façade connects the different volumes in the complex, which cover an area of 7,140 m² (77,000 sq ft).

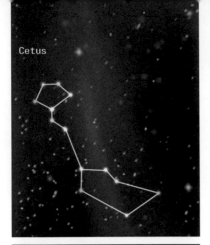

Cetus

Thom Mayne

© Reiner Zettl

Morphosis
2041 Colorado Avenue
Santa Monica, CA 90404, USA
Tel.: +1 310 453 2247
www.morphosis.net

Thom Mayne was born in Waterbury, Connecticut, in 1942 and graduated with an architecture degree from the University of Southern California in 1969. He was a founder of the Southern California Institute of Architecture and has held teaching positions at Cal Poly Pomona and UCLA. In 1972 he founded Morphosis together with Michael Rotondi. The practice currently has offices in Los Angeles and New York. He received the prestigious Pritzker Prize in March 2005. Among other acknowlegments for his work are the 2001 Chrysler Design Award of Excellence and the 1992 Brunner Prize in Architecture.

## Wayne L. Morse United States Courthouse
Eugene, OR, USA / 2006 / Photos: © Nic Lehoux

This courthouse complex has six levels and 25,000 m² (269,097 sq ft) of floor space. It also contains two offices for the US senators elected by the State of Oregon. The volume features curving lines and an atrium with a height of 26 m (85 ft).

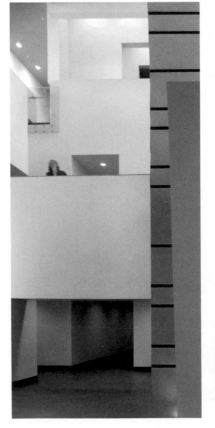

The building received LEED certification for sustainability and energy saving.

The steel mesh enveloping a large part of this building makes it a far cry from the typical simple and drab designs of district schools. The remodeling of this industrial building dating from 1912 and the addition of two floors is a model conversion.

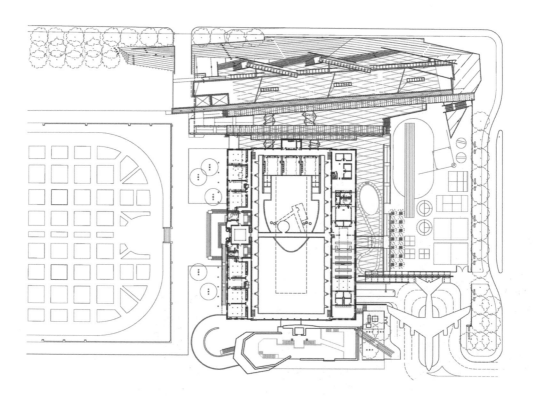

Translucent metal dividers become a unifying element for different areas of the project.

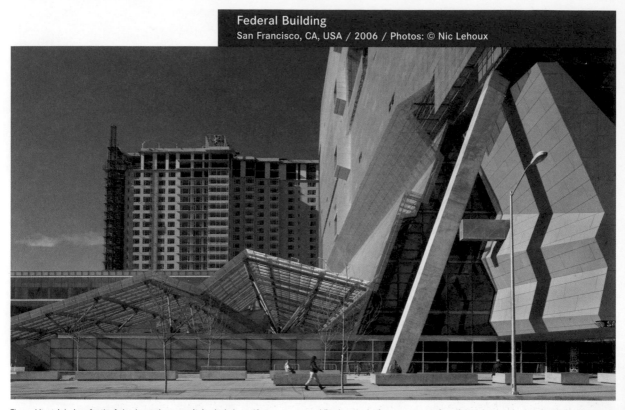

The architects' designs for the federal complex commission include an 18-story tower, a public plaza, and a four-story annex. One of the primary objectives for the interiors was to democratize the work spaces to guarantee equal conditions for all departments.

The carefully thought-out design means that 90 percent of work spaces have natural light and access to windows that open.

This project, in addition to offering students public spaces, creates transit flows between the different and previously poorly connected buildings, with the aim of resuming social commitments.

The volume houses recreation spaces, classrooms, student housing, a dining hall, and a store.

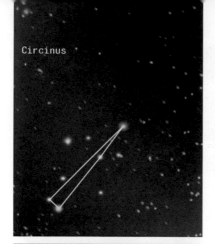

Circinus

## Wolf D. Prix

© Elfie Semotan

Coop Himmelb(l)au
Spengergasse, 37
1050 Vienna, Austria
Tel.: +43 1 546 60 0
www.coop-himmelblau.at

Wolf D. Prix founded the Coop Himmelb(l)au
practice in association with Helmut Swiczinsky
and Michael Holzer in Vienna in 1968. The Los
Angeles office was opened 20 years later. With
such important projects as the East Pavilion of
the Groninger Museum, the UFA Cinema Center in Dresden, and the Academy of Fine Arts
in Munich, the firm has become one of the
most prestigious in Europe. This statement is
backed by acknowledgments such as the RIBA
Award for the BMW Welt project, and the 2007
International Architecture Award.

## BMW Welt
Munich, Germany / 2007 / Photos: © Ari Marcopoulos

The auto maker BMW wanted a building with an overwhelming design, for the delivery of 250 cars each day. The design of the building, with its curved forms and double cone characterizing the structure, seems to contribute to its role as a delivery center.

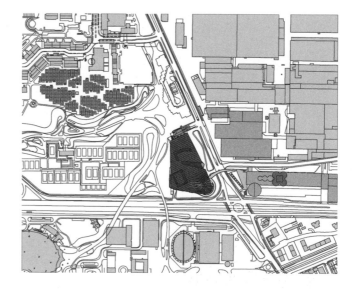

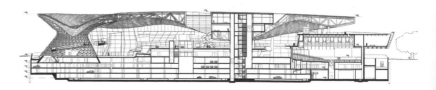

456

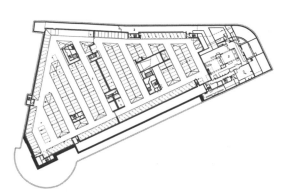

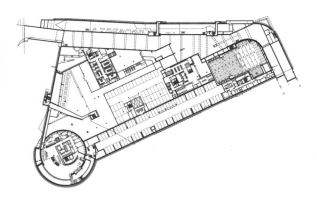

Molded concrete makes the free-form shapes possible. From among the metamorphic materials used in construction, the entrance features crystalline silica.

The new headquarters of the European Central Bank will be located in the Ostend district of Frankfurt. With a total height of 185 m (607 ft), this double polygonal tower will become an architectural landmark for the city.

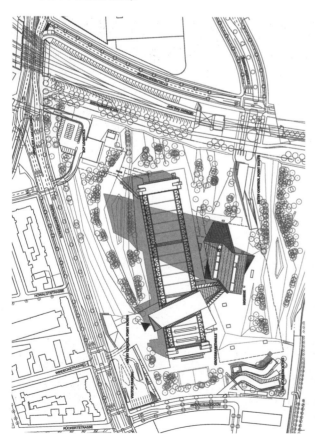

The broken planes of the façade keep a certain correspondence with the interior beams.

This high school is located very near to the cathedral designed by Rafael Moneo for the city of Los Angeles, on Grand Avenue, and contains a theater with a capacity for close to 1,000 people. The classrooms are laid out in four independent volumes.

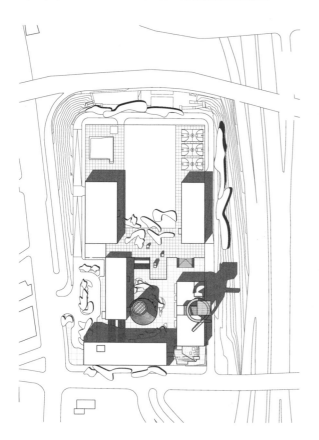

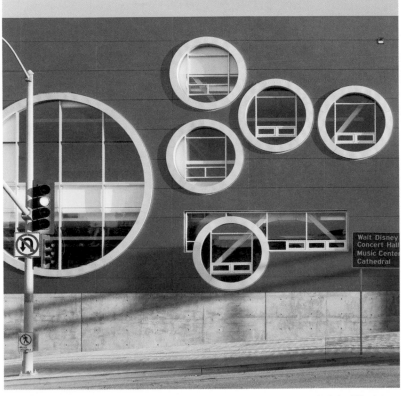

The windows on some of the façades seem to form abstract pictures and become the project's distinguishing feature.

Corvus

## Gurjit Singh Matharoo

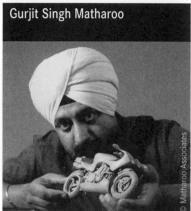

© Matharoo Associates

Matharoo Associates
24/E, Capital Commercial Centre
Ashram Road, Ahmedabad 380-009
Gujarat, India
Tel.: +91 79 2657 7757
www.matharooassociates.com

With a workforce of 15, the firm founded by Gurjit Singh Matharoo in 1991 undertakes architecture, interior design, product design and structural design work. With frequent forays into atypical disciplines, Matharoo has designed vans and mopeds. In his more habitual work, he has received acknowledgments such as the Architectural Review International Emerging Architecture Award in 2003 and 2005. In India, he also received the J. K. Cement Award as the best young architect of the year in 2001 and 2002.

## Sainik School
Balachadi, India / 2005 / Photos: © Joginder Singh

This military school is raised around a strict grid of columns that envelop a large central courtyard. From the outside, the façades form patterns with continuous openings that give the complex a lighter feel.

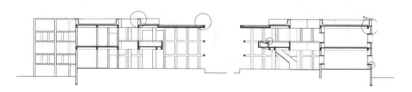

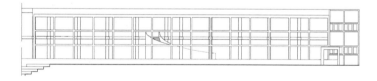

The volume rises from a depression in the terrain, which explains the terraced forecourt.

**Dilip Sanghvi**

Surat, India / To be determined / Photos: © Matharoo Associates, Dinesh Mehta

The design of this single-family home combines features of the most contemporary international residential architecture, as seen in its façade, and elements inherent to Indian design, visible in the colorful and almost maximalist style of the interior.

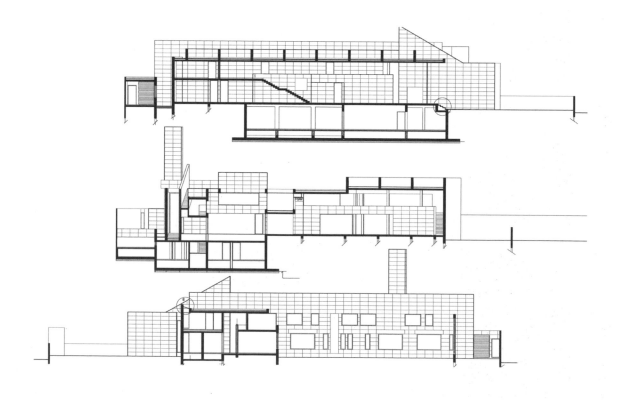

The main element of the interior is precast concrete panels, over which work is carried out with ornamental details.

Delphinus

## Bolle Tham
## & Martin Videgård Hansson

© Tham & Videgård Hansson Arkitekter

**Tham & Videgård Hansson Arkitekter**
**Blekingegatan, 46**
**116 62 Stockholm, Sweden**
**Tel.: +46 8 702 00 46**
**www.tvh.se**

Bolle Tham and Martin Videgård Hansson founded their practice in 1999. In 2007 they were chosen by *Wallpaper* as one of the ten most interesting new architects, and their projects such as the Kalmar Museum of Art have been nominated for awards such as the Mies van der Rohe. This very work received the Helgo Zetterval Prize in 2008. The founding partners of the firm have taught at the Stuttgart School of Architecture, and their project for the Archipelago house was nominated for the prize for best Swedish wooden building in 2008.

## Archipelago House
Stockholm, Sweden / 2006 / Photos: © Åke E:son Lindman

Designed as a light wood and glass structure, this summer house is located in one of the rockiest parts of the Stockholm Archipelago. The floor plan is determined by the features of the site, as it is set between large rocks.

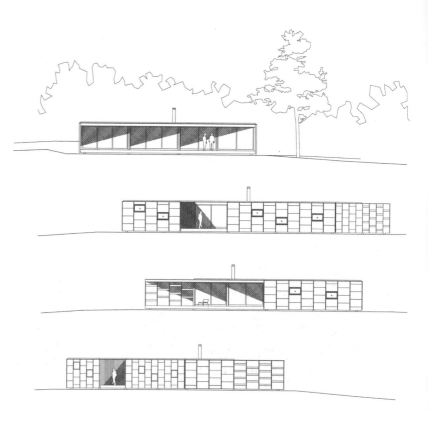

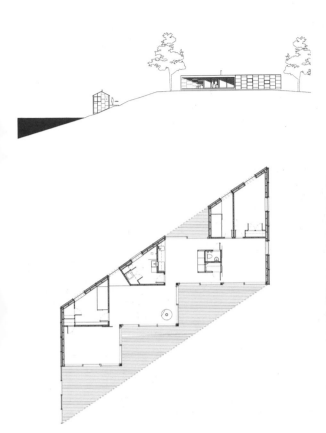

The zigzag floor plan becomes a distinguishing feature of the house.

This residence is laid out as a spiral sequence of four spacious rooms on four levels. The façade features protruding wooden boxes containing windows.

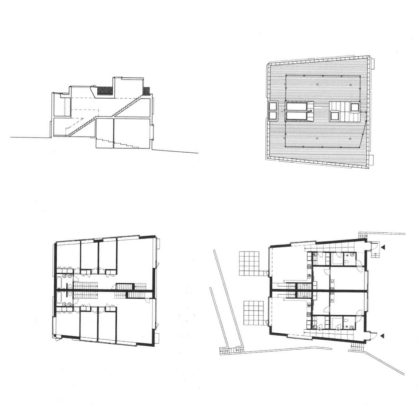

The abrupt cuts and continuous openings and cavities are features of the different rooms.

**Karlsson House**
Västerås, Sweden / 2002 / Photos: © Åke E:son Lindman

Located on the north shore of Lake Mälaren in central Sweden, this house recreates the traditional simplicity characterizing houses in the area. This made the task easy given that it also had to be built on a limited budget.

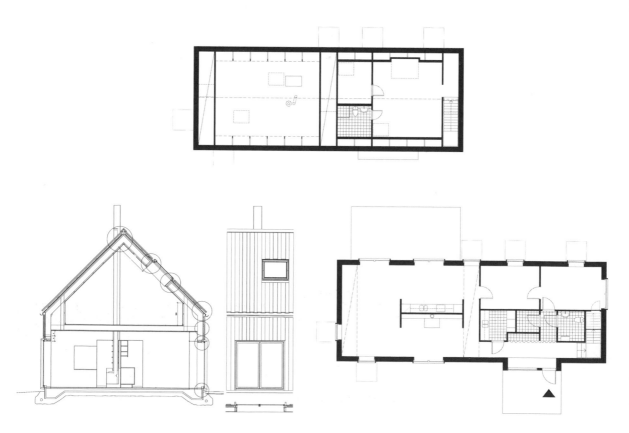

In contrast with the dark red façade, the interiors are airy and open plan.

Winner of an international design competition, the project for the Kalmar Museum of Art consists of a black cube on four levels, featuring large wooden panels interrupted by ample glass expanses, and with two main spaces: the white box and the top floor gallery.

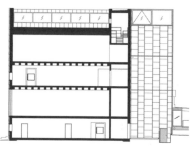

The interior features exposed concrete walls combined with panels of black treated wood.

This home located in the Stocksund district comprises a simple perforated block that allows light to penetrate, and features double heights and a roof terrace. The façades are clad in black plywood panels.

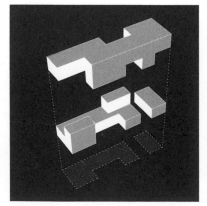

The interiors are finished in white dry walling, matching the color of the floors.

Canes Venatici

## Renzo Piano

© Stefano Goldberg

**Renzo Piano Building Workshop**
Via Rubens, 29
16158 Genova, Italy
Tel.: +39 010 61 711
www.rpbw.com

Renzo Piano was born in Genoa in 1937 into a family of builders. He studied at the Polytechnic University of Milan, a city where he also worked in Franco Albini's studio. He graduated in 1964. In 1971 he founded Piano & Rogers with Richard Rogers, with whom he won the design competition for the Centre Pompidou in Paris, the city where he currently lives. In 1981 he founded Renzo Piano Building Workshop, a firm with over 100 employees and offices in Paris, Genoa, and New York. Among his most prestigious awards are the Pritzker Prize, the Sonning Prize and the AIA Gold Medal.

## Morgan Library Extension
New York, NY, USA / 2006 / Photos: © Michel Denancé

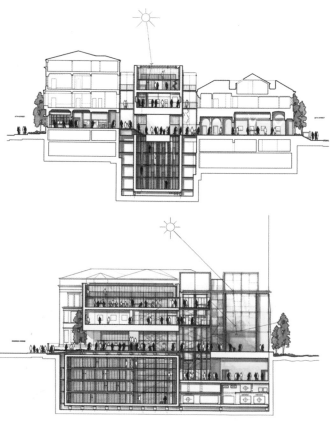

Both library and cultural center, this site houses the J. P. Morgan Collection, one of the world's most impressive collection of medieval and renaissance manuscripts, including music manuscripts. The extension was largely carried out underground, although the new atrium is an outstanding feature.

The pre-existing building's interior was also remodeled to allow better use to be made of the museum's collections.

The new headquarters of one of the important newspapers in the world is an almost transparent 52-story building that is very permeable to the transit of its occupants. Instead of a fashionable mirror glass façade, the glass is translucent and turns blue after rain and a reddish hue at sunset.

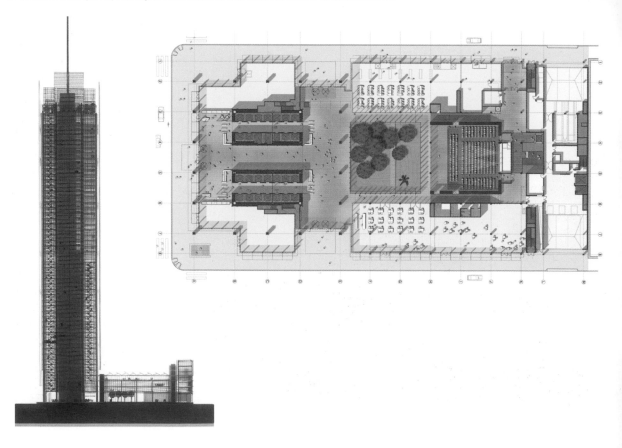

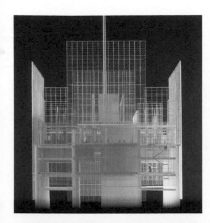

The lobby and large internal garden are publicly accessible, confirming the public service nature of the building.

## California Academy of Sciences
San Francisco, CA, USA / 2008 / Photos: © Tim Griffith

The new building of this cultural institution is located on the same site and keeps the same orientation as the former buildings. It is also laid out around a large central piazza. The roof unifies the functions of the volume and features 55,000 photovoltaic cells generating energy for the entire complex.

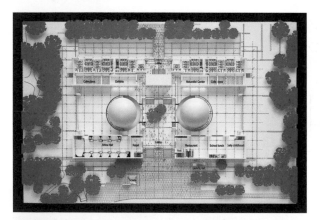

A large skylight illuminates the central atrium and gives it the appearance of a semi-exterior space.

## Jaime Varon, Abraham Metta & Alex Metta

© Migdal Arquitectos

Migdal Arquitectos
Av. de la Prolongación
Paseo de la Reforma, 1236, piso 11
Colonia Santa Fe
Delegación Cuajimalpa
05348 Mexico City, Mexico
Tel.: +52 55 9177 0177
www.migdal.com.mx

Commissioned for integral development projects, Migdal Arquitectos specializes in the different disciplines related to architecture. With over 20 years of experience, the firm has completed more than 280 projects, among them residential complexes (including social housing), office buildings, retail complexes and industrial parks. Their most outstanding work includes the Gota de Plata Auditorium, a large theater located in the Mexican state of Hidalgo.

## Atrio Interlomas
Huixquilucan, Mexico / 2009 / Photos: © Alex Giribet

This project is based on the idea of a large central courtyard of over 8,700 m² (93,650 sq ft). The distances between the different towers are considerable, enabling a large area to be developed as green space.

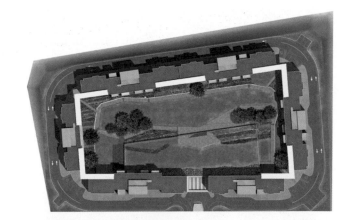

In addition to the residential towers, the project includes a swimming pool and two underground levels of parking and storage units.

This building with a continuous form acts as a pinnacle in an area with high-rise buildings. The distinguishing feature of the design is that it offers the best vantage point over the city, given that the perimeter belts framing the windows enhance the panoramic views.

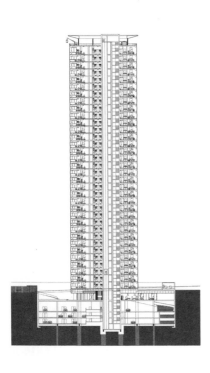

The project was developed in association with the LAR Fernando Romero studio.

This residential building takes the form of a boomerang to create a concave interior space opening out to the urban frontage on Paseo de la Reforma, one of the Mexico City's main thoroughfares. The building folds, opens and encompasses the great square with its statue of Columbus.

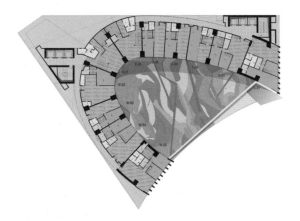

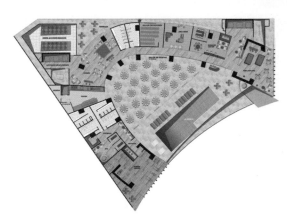

The corners of the building are accentuated through the placement of vertical elements that enhance the feeling of height.

Six large concrete elements form the backbone of the building and support the roofing system. A large frame involving an armor-beam completes the building. This innovative process for building the frame provides necessary stability to the entire structural system.

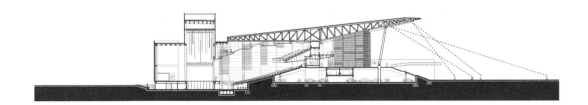

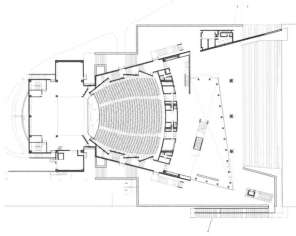

One of the main features is the cantilevered roof that houses an anchoring system for hundreds of glass and mirror sheets.

Located in the north of Mexico City, Tres Lagos is a residential complex comprising 11 towers, 10 with 13 stories and 1 with 7, in addition to a two-level multi-purpose building. Positioned to create broad garden spaces, the towers feature an attractive overlay of skins.

The project is centered on a large garden that serves as a meeting place.

Monoceros

Thomas Herzog

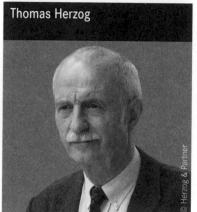

© Herzog & Partner

## Mountain Rescue Center
Bergwacht Bayern, Germany / 2008 / Photos: © Christoph Stepan

The aim of the architect in this project was to create a large transparent space containing a simulation facility for training rescue teams, which can also be used by police and firefighters.

Herzog & Partner
Imhofstrasse, 3 A
80805 Munich, Germany
Tel.: +49 89 36057 0
www.herzog-und-partner.de

Thomas Herzog was born in 1941 in Munich. He studied architecture at the city's Technical University between 1960 and 1965. Over the four following years he worked as assistant to Professor C. von Seideln, and he received his doctorate from the University of Rome in 1972. He founded his own architectural practice in 1971, which has won such important awards as the 1981 Mies van der Rohe, the 2007 Chicago Athenaeum International Architecture Award, and the 2008 IBS (International Building Skin-Tech) Award. He has also taught at universities in Kassel, Darmstadt and Munich (where he was also the dean of the Faculty of Architecture at the Technical University).

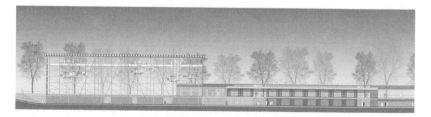

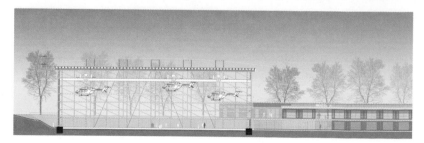

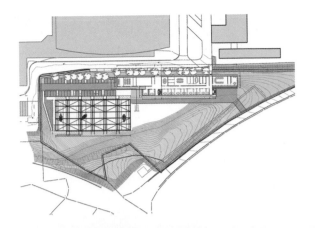

The close to 20 m (65 ft) height provides large capacity for the interior. The structure is also resistant to wind and avalanches.

This building, one of the world's largest data processing centers, houses a large central computer. The site was required to comply with a very specific set of requirements, which, extraordinarily, did not take away from its architectural identity.

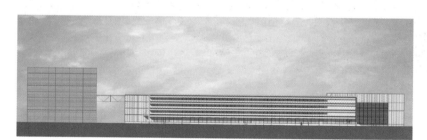

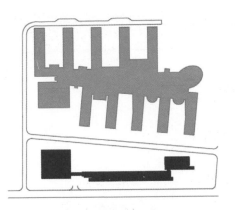

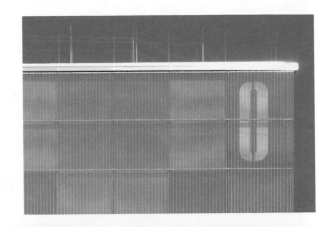

The metal block is 27.50 m (90 ft) tall and 35 m (115 ft) long.

The façade of this modern office building features the installation of an innovative system of louvers that magnify sunlight to save on lighting costs. Another function of the façade is to preheat the incoming air so as to lower energy use in heating.

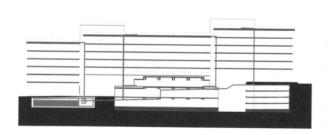

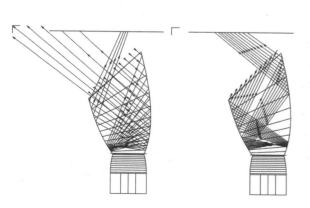

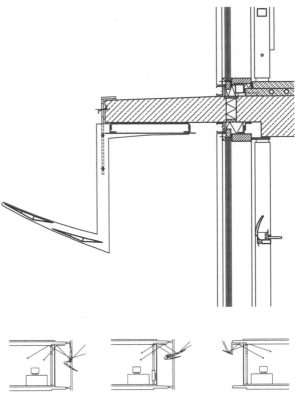

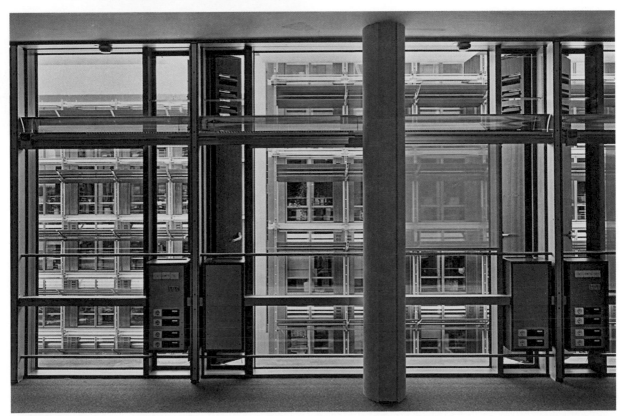

The louvers running the length of the façade become a strong decorative element.

Leo

Gert Wingårdh

© Wingårdh Arkitektkontor AB

## House of Sweden / Washington D. C., USA
2006 / Photos: © Åke E:son Lindman, Patrik Gunnar Helin

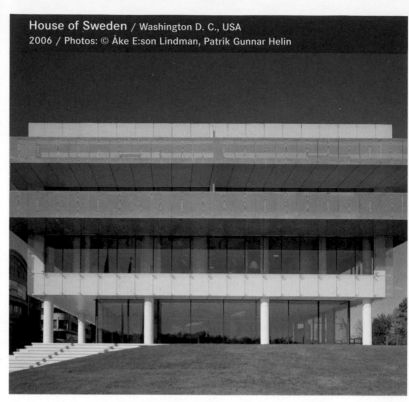

This office building has six levels and a roof terrace, in addition to an underground parking garage. The entrance is located at the same level as that of the highest flood waters expected on the Potomac River.

Wingårdh Arkitektkontor AB
Kungsgatan, 10 A
SE 411 19 Göteborg, Sweden
Tel.: +46 31 743 70 00
www.wingardhs.se

Gert Wingårdh established his own architectural practice in 1977. It started by accepting minor commissions from stores, restaurants and individuals. Gradually institutional work came on a larger scale, reaching the importance of those currently being designed, like the winning project for the new Olympic stadium in Stockholm. Acknowledgment has come in the form of numerous awards, among which are six Kasper Salin Awards and one ESCN European Award for Excellence in the use of concrete, in 2002.

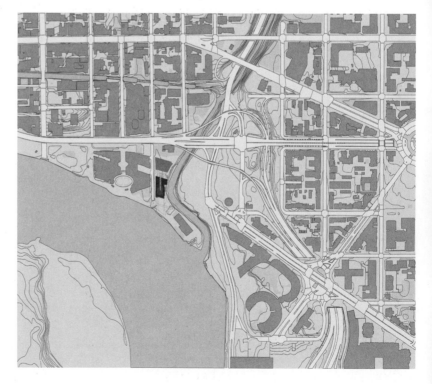

As an official building, it was important that it gave a feel of transparency, which led to its open design.

Located beside the autobahn connecting Rostock with Berlin, the Müritzeum is a national park with seven lakes, one of which is the largest in Germany. This building serves as a lookout over the lake and features a curved façade, which seems to form a kind of "vertical shore."

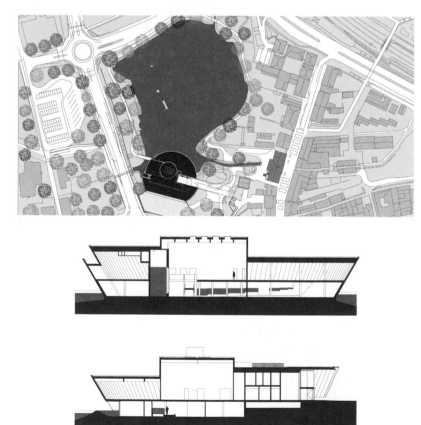

The dark finishing is in perfect harmony with the surrounding landscape.

The basic design of this project was established by placing a series of rooms in a straight line. Facing west to the sea, the only thing separating the interior from the outside world is a continuous 10 mm (0.4 in) thick glass membrane.

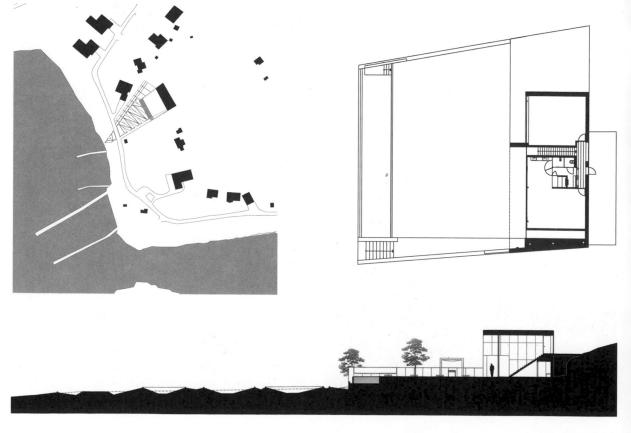

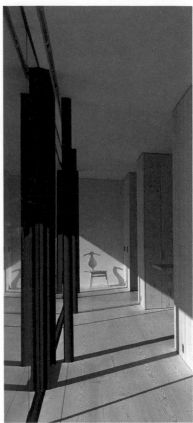

Except for the glass screen, the rest of the façade is an elegantly-finished, very slightly textured concrete.

This department store is part of the renewal of the commercial area of the Stockholm suburb of Vällingby. The combination of white glass and electric red cladding make it a powerful advertising symbol in its own right.

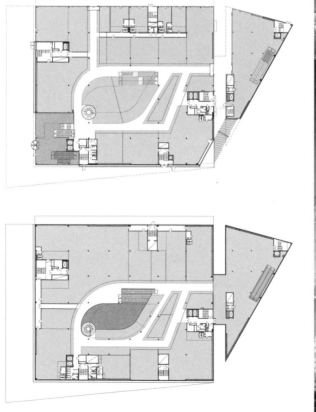

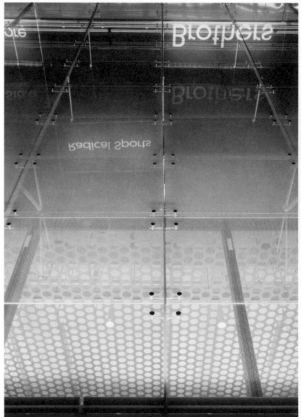

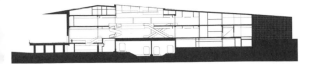

Visually striking interiors were essential to guarantee customer loyalty.

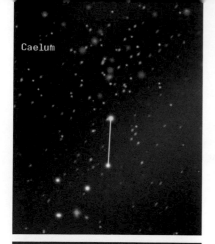

Caelum

Helmut Jahn

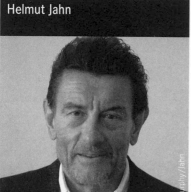

© Murphy/Jahn

Murphy/Jahn
35 East Wacker Drive, 3rd floor
Chicago, IL 60601, USA
Tel.: +1 312 427 7300
www.murphyjahn.com

Helmut Jahn was born in Nuremberg, Germany, in 1940. He graduated from the Technical University of Munich in 1965 and later took postgraduate studies at the Illinois Institute of Technology. He worked as assistant to Gene Summers at Murphy Associates and in 1982 became the president of Murphy/Jahn. He has taught at universities such as Yale and the Illinois Institute of Technology. He has received awards such as the DuPont Benedictus, the Bund Deutscher Architekten, and countless AIA awards for his works in Chicago.

## Suvarnabhumi International Airport
Bangkok, Thailand / 2006 / Photos: © Rainer Viertlböck

Based on the studio's 50 years of airport design experience, this airport is outstanding in its understanding of the correct layout of open spaces. It was important for the architect to guarantee spatial optimization, for which he designed the airport as a mini city.

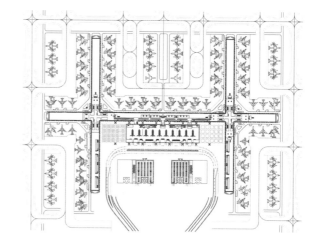

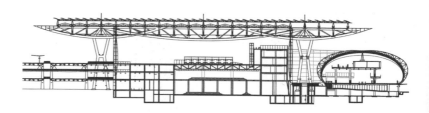

Ultra-light metal and solid precast concrete structures enabled a skin to be created that covers most of the airport facilities.

This university residential complex comprises three five-story buildings. A reinforced concrete frame buffers them from noise and vibrations from the elevated train tracks that run behind the site. Glass sheet and stainless steel cladding act as a screen, adding to this insulation and blocking unsightly views.

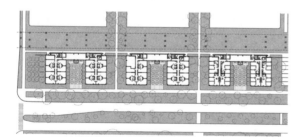
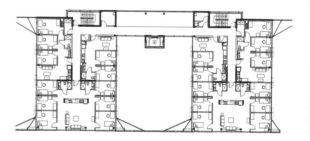

The continuous wall structure curves at roof height and gives way to vaulted metal canopies that provide partial shade for the roof terraces.

As often happens with Murphy/Jahn's large-scale projects, the interior of this trade exhibition center resembles a city. The halls form a triangle to create the core exhibition area, connected to different passageways lined with stores.

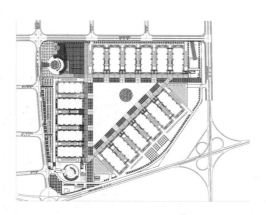

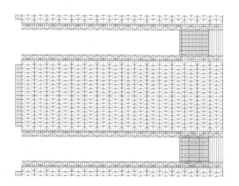

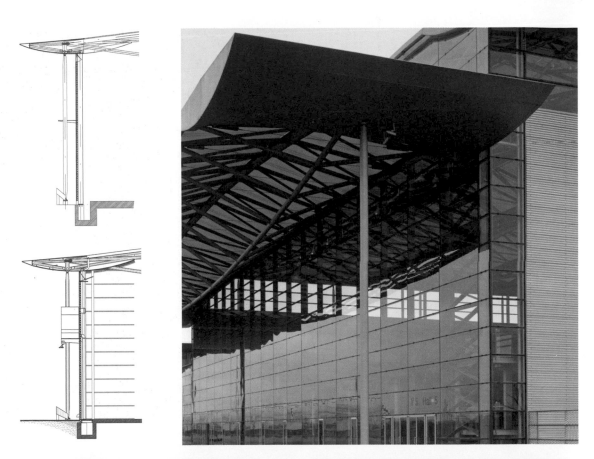

The column-and obstacle-free halls are 11 m (36 ft) high, although the largest has a ceiling height of 17 m (56 ft).

## Deutsche Post Tower
Bonn, Germany / 2003 / Photos: © Andreas Keller

Rising 162 m (530 ft), this tower was designed with a pleasing oval shape, split in half and shifted to form sharp angles. The two half-cylinders are separated by a space more than 7 m (23 ft) wide, and are connected by bridge floors every nine levels.

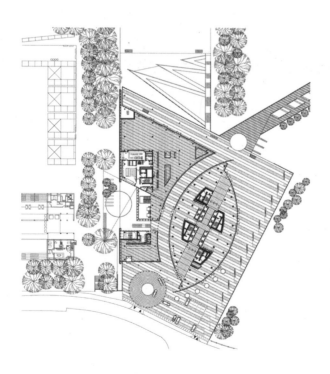

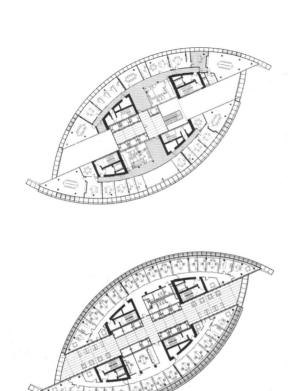

The façade is a single shade of blue, but takes on different colors at night by means of a sophisticated LED point lighting system.

Canes Venatici

## Astrid Klein
## & Mark Dytham

© Klein Dytham architecture

## Uniqlo
Tokyo, Japan / 2005 / Photos: © Nacasa & Partners

Located in the bustling commercial thoroughfare that is Ginza, the façade of this building essentially functions as an advertisement, given that the LED system works like a giant low-res video screen. As Uniqlo is Japan's equivalent of The Gap, the low-res façade was a reaction to the low price/good value brand message.

**KDa—Klein Dytham architecture**
**AD Building 2F, 1-15-7 Hiroo**
**Shibuya-ku**
**Tokyo 150-0012, Japan**
**www.klein-dytham.com**

Klein Dytham architecture (KDa) is a multi-disciplinary design practice (not only specializing in architecture but also in interiors and installations) based in Japan and led by Astrid Klein and Mark Dytham, who founded the firm in 1991. Not having a specific prescriptive style, KDa prefers to find inspiration from their dealings with clients, which explains the diverse and cheerful nature of their projects. With increasingly more important commissions, the practice exudes a cosmopolitan spirit that is present in its buildings.

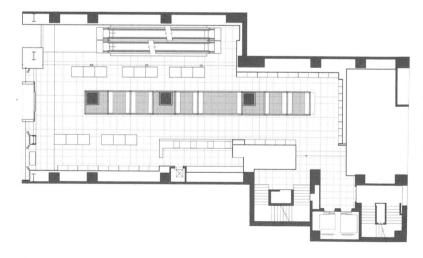

The brand logo shines through the building's frontage by means of high power LED lights, which adds another layer to the pixellated façade.

## Nagoya Flat
Nagoya, Japan / 2004 / Photos: © Katsuhisa Kida

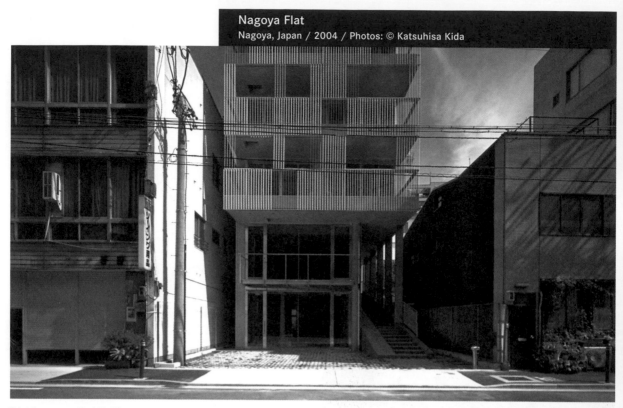

This tall, narrow residential building, a common occurrence in Japan, has a screen made up of vertical balustrades coated with polarized paint. The balustrades connect to create a continuous screen masking the usually heavy balcony set backs.

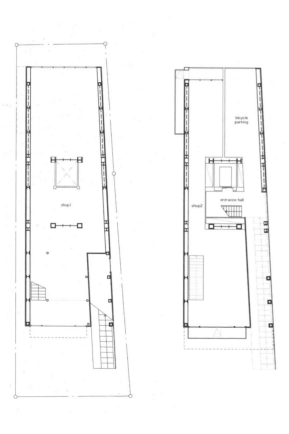

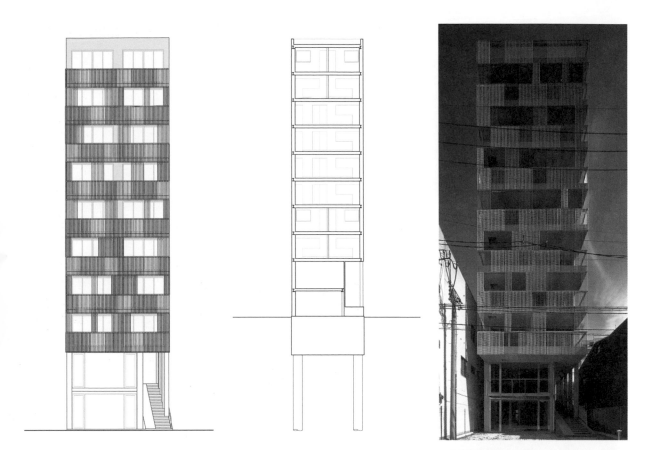

The stainless steel louvers of the balustrades are coated with a pearlescent two tone paint which changes hue depending on viewing angle and the position of the sun.

Surrounded by the grounds of the Risonare Hotel, this chapel is formed by two leaves, one of steel and the other of glass. The glass leaf is supported on a steel structure rather like the veins of a leaf.

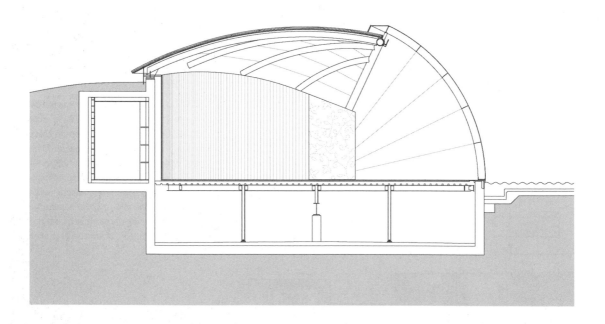

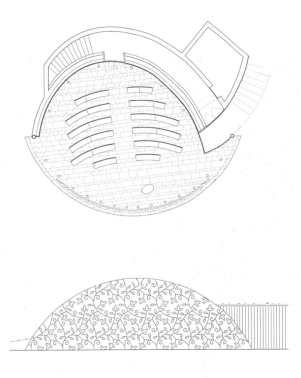

Perforated with 4,700 holes, each fitted with an acrylic lens, the steel leaf resembles a bride's veil and rises open at the end of the wedding ceremony.

Designed for a young couple and their baby, this project integrates a residence and a hair salon run by the owners. A striking black box contains the living spaces, which can be seen through frameless windows.

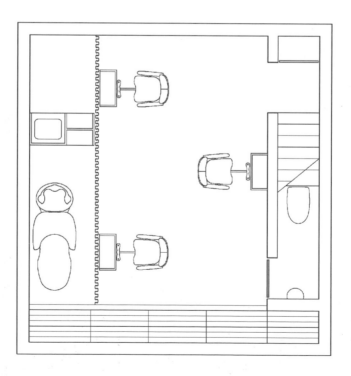

The exterior "embroidery" adds personality to the house and advertises the salon.

# Wilson House

Chiba, Japan / 2008 / Photos: © Daici Ano

Covering 230 m² (2,475 sq ft), this house was designed so that the interiors could take the best advantage of the impressive views surrounding the site. A spacious balcony runs the length of the main façade, which is completely glassed.

There is a semi-exterior space on the lower level, which is prepared for new rooms in the future.

Located in an inner-city district of the Japanese capital, this house features a simple but visually attractive wooden frame and plywood panels, clad externally with a simple glazing system.

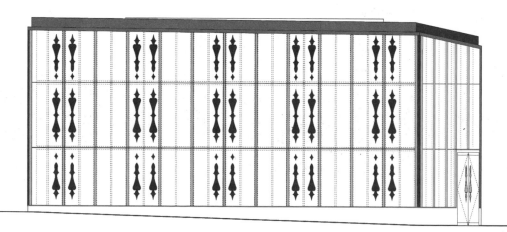

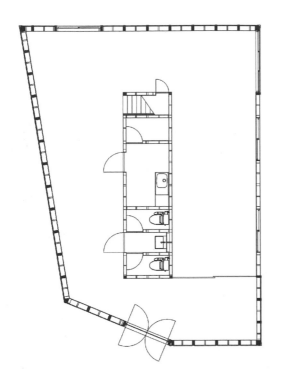

This project seems aimed at architects—the glass cladding showing how the building was constructed.

Hercules

## Urs Bette

© Margit Brünner

Urs Bette Architecture
116 Margaret Street
North Adelaide, SA 5006, Australia
Tel.: +61 8 8267 4618
www.bette.at

Urs Bette studied design in Düsseldorf in 1992 and completed a degree in architecture at the University of Applied Arts in Vienna in 2000. He worked for the Coop Himmelb(l)au firm before setting up his own studio in 2002. Bette has taught and coordinated courses at the Faculty of Architecture at the University of Adelaide, and his work has been featured in publications such as *Architects Directory*, *Arch+*, and *Wallpaper*.

## Pavilion for Expo 2010
Shanghai, China / 2010 / Renderings: © Urs Bette

This project for the Austrian pavilion at Expo 2010, to be held in Shanghai, has capacity for 63 pieces of a collection—musical instruments in this case—that come to different places in Austria. As a result, the pavilion represents a giant music box.

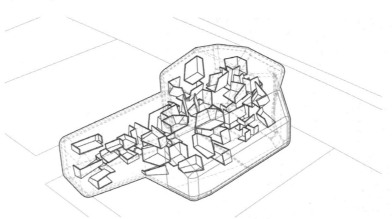

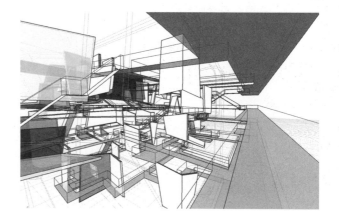

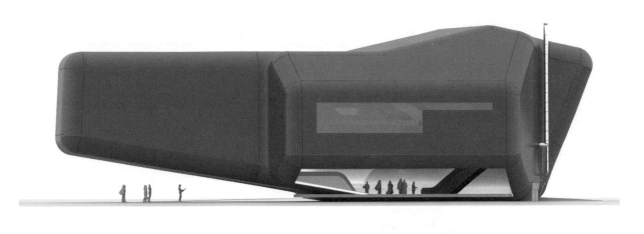

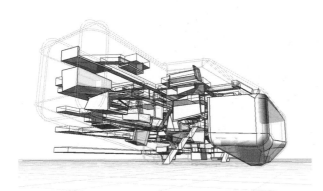

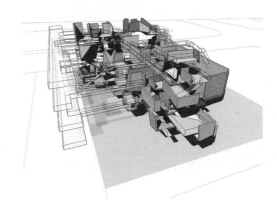

The curved lines of the interior walls form a negative image of the structure created by the façade.

Futuristic looks and striking metal cladding on the exterior define this impressive residential development project. The different volumes are supported by pillars to make the best use of the sloping terrain, giving rise to platforms that serve as viewing decks.

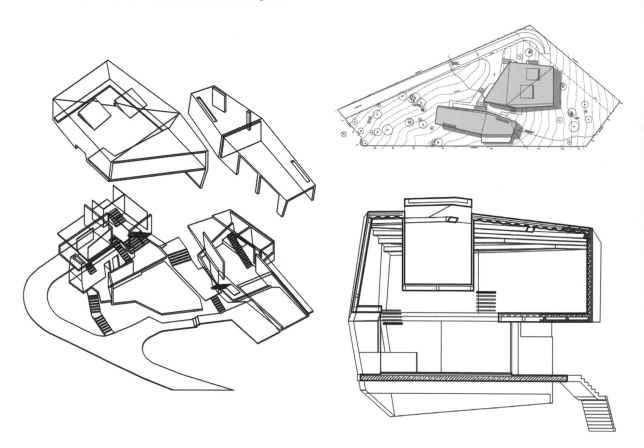

Interior light comes from unusual sources such as doors and stairwells.

Antlia

Daniel Libeskind

© Studio Daniel Libeskind

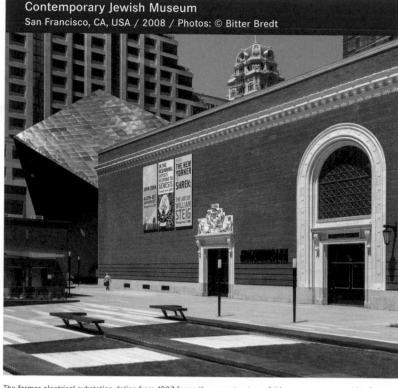

## Contemporary Jewish Museum
San Francisco, CA, USA / 2008 / Photos: © Bitter Bredt

The former electrical substation dating from 1907 forms the core structure of this new museum, to which Daniel Libeskind has added a protective layer of over 3,000 blue steel panels. This new skin seems to change its color and intensity depending on the solar exposure.

**Studio Daniel Libeskind**
2 Rector Street, 19th floor
New York, NY 10006, USA
Tel.: +1 212 497 9100
www.daniel-libeskind.com

Daniel Libeskind, born in Lódz, Poland, in 1946, was a musician before becoming an architect. Internationally-acclaimed, his work is typified by the multi-disciplinary approach he takes to his projects. Outstanding among his works are the Jewish Museum Berlin, the Imperial War Museum North in Manchester, and the more recent work at the Denver Art Museum. Acknowledgments include the 1999 Deutsche Architekturpreis, the 2000 Goethe Medal and the 2001 Hiroshima Art Prize. He has taught at the University of Pennsylvania and Yale.

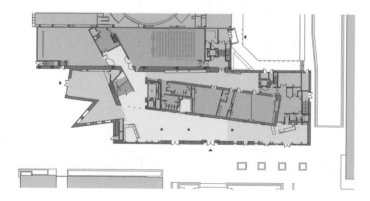

The dimensions of the former substation offer the perfect interior spaces for showing works of art.

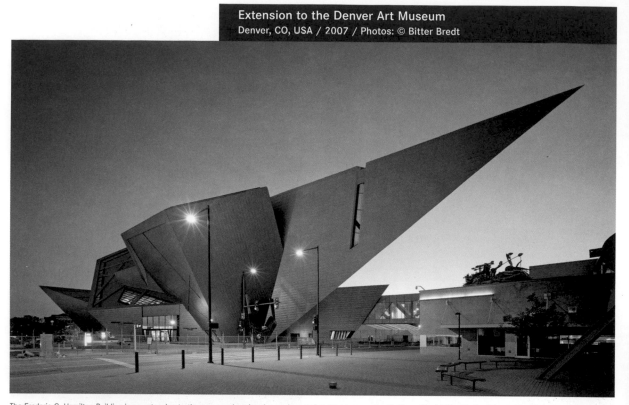

The Frederic C. Hamilton Building is an extension to the museum housing the modern and contemporary art collections. Daniel Libeskind collaborated with the Davis Partnership on the design of this iconic building. The project combined locally-sourced stone with modern materials like titanium.

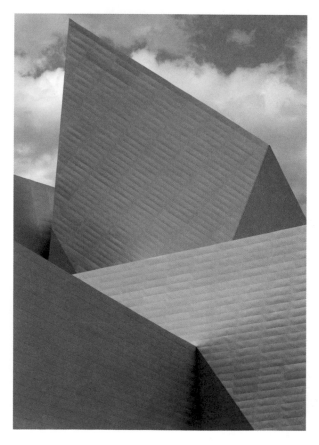

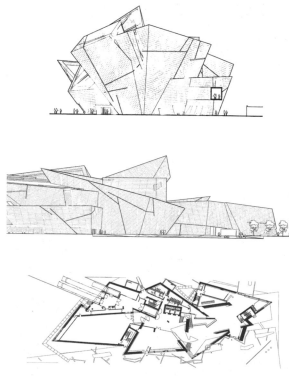

This structure was not designed as a building, but as a series of public spaces full of vitality.

With 55 stores, 10 restaurants, a water park, a wellness center and mutiplex cinemas, the impact of this complex comes from its dramatic position over a major highway. The innovative structure is the main feature of the center with the overwhelming number of sharp angles that are characteristic of the architect's work. It also stands as a gateway to the city.

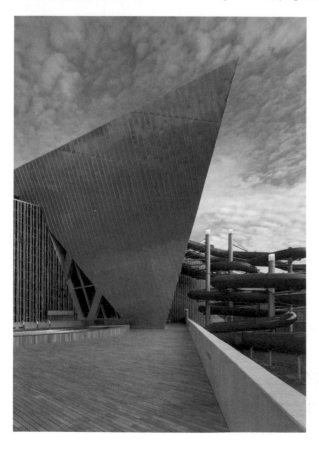

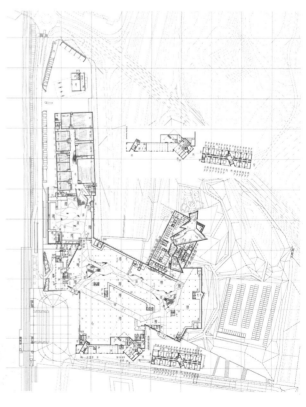

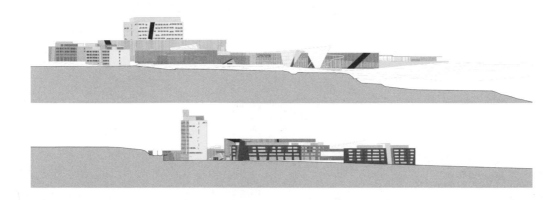

Bernaqua is the largest spa in Switzerland. The center features angles reminiscent of images from expressionist movies.

The Wohl Centre is a convention center built as part of the extensions to the Bar-Ilan University. Sculpted in the shape of an open book, the building becomes a "labyrinth of letters" clad in golden metal. The structure's impact comes mainly from the visual continuity of its shapes.

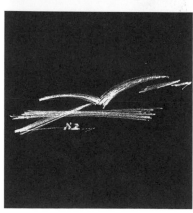

The interior is a strategy of violently contrasting planes, typical of Daniel Libeskind's designs.

Draco

## Tristán Diéguez & Áxel Fridman

Diéguez Fridman Arquitectos
& Asociados
Álvarez Thomas, 198
1427 Buenos Aires, Argentina
Tel.: +54 11 4551 9900
www.dieguezfridman.com.ar

Tristán Diéguez was born in Buenos Aires in 1972. He graduated from the University of Buenos Aires in 1997 and worked for the prestigious firm of Cesar Pelli from 1998 to 2008. A year older, Axel Fridman is also from Buenos Aires. In 1998 he graduated with a master's degree in Advanced Architectural Design from Columbia University. They founded their own firm in 2000 and received their first important commission in 2004 for a building to house the University of Buenos Aires' School of Economics. Their star on the national and international architectural scene has not ceased to rise since then.

## Huaxi Urban Center

Guiyang, China / To be determined / Renderings: © Diéguez Fridman

This building is designed as a spiral that emerges from the first level as a series of steps of differing sizes. This spiral is perforated by living spaces and connects interior and exterior zones.

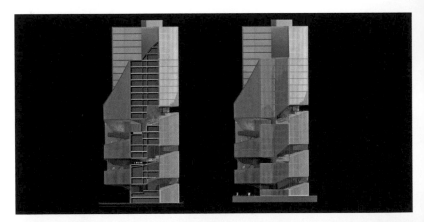

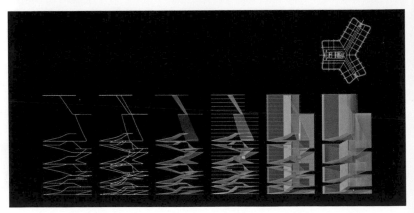

The main objective of the project was to link the tower to the uneven terrain of the site.

This futuristic residence, one of 100 villas commissioned by a Chinese developer from 100 renowned architects, offers different spatial conditions in a single volume: sunken spaces in contact with nature, vertical spaces with views of the sky, and raised areas that overlook the exterior.

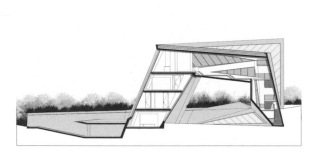

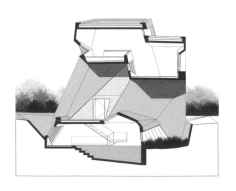

The interior spaces are laid out over four levels.

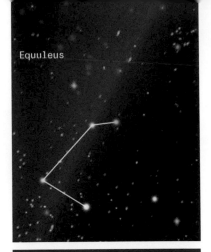

Equuleus

## Robert Konieczny

© Juliusz Sokołowski

KWK Promes
Ul. Rymera, 3-5
40-061 Katowice, Poland
Tel.: +48 32 206 91 26
www.kwkpromes.pl

Born in 1969 in Katowice, Poland, Robert Konieczny studied at the New Jersey Institute of Technology and the Silesian University of Technology in Gliwice. He founded KWK Promes in 1999 together with Marlena Wolnik, who formed part of the firm until 2005. In 2007 Konieczny was chosen by *Wallpaper* magazine as one of the 101 most interesting new architects and received awards such as the Leonardo 2007, in addition to several nominations for the Mies van der Rohe Award. In 2008 his name joined the prestigious Europe 40 Under 40 list.

## Aatrial House
Lower Silesia, Poland / 2006 / Photos: © Juliusz Sokołowski, Aleksander Rutkowski

Located on a 1 hectare (2.5 acre) site adjoining a leafy forest, the design of this residence solves the problem of a badly-oriented driveway (south-west direction) coming into conflict with the location for the garden. The architect raised the lower level of the house above the driveway.

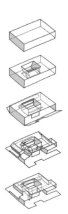

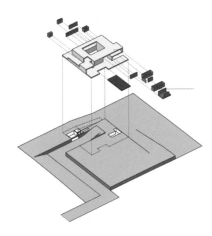

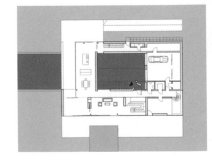

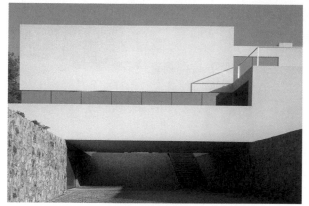

The way the house is raised makes it the contrary of a building that is based around an atrium, from which it takes its name.

The structural design of this house is formed by a series of rectangular solids, which contrast with the ribbon-like structure that winds around them like a frame after emerging from the ground.

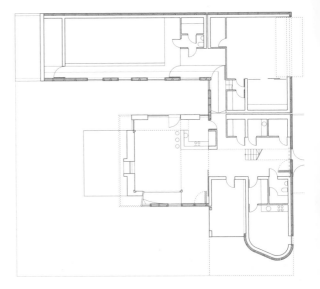

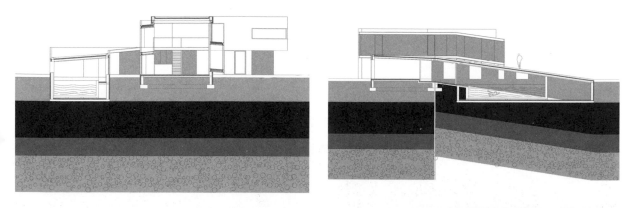

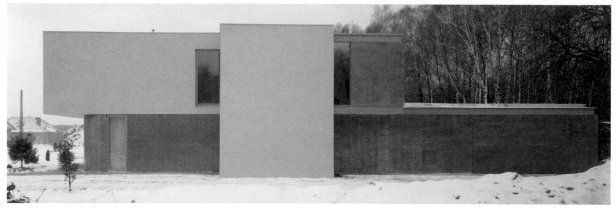

The ocher ribbon that envelops the house is prolonged in the access ramp, a visual reference of the design.

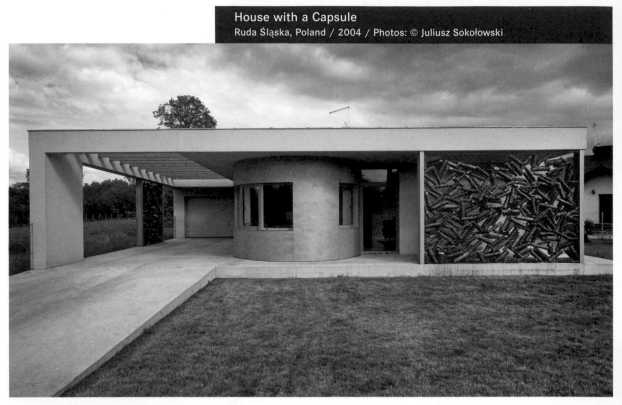

The large metal beam that acts as a frame for the façade of this house has a dramatic effect while helping to divide the different interior and exterior spaces clearly.

Ovals and right angles are masterfully combined throughout the structure to create a modern feel of diversity.

## Outrial House
### Ksążenice, Poland / 2007 / Photos: © Juliusz Sokołowski

Designed for a limited budget and with the idea of low maintenance, this residence was built partially buried into the site, enabling the creation of interesting gardens that are roofs at the same time.

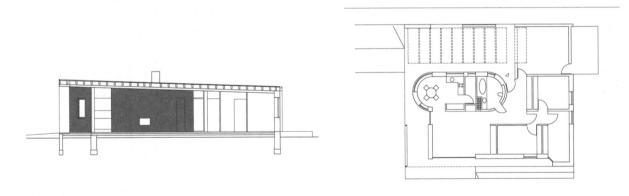

The lower level, lying close to the level of the ground, benefits from contact with the exterior spaces, despite their small size.

Most of the dwellings in the region where this project is located are villas with steep gabled roofs. This is why the design of this residence is so distinct—hidden underground and with a trapdoor disguising the entrance.

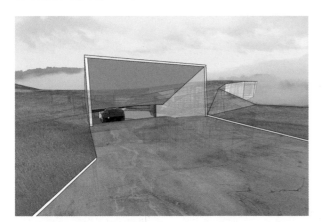

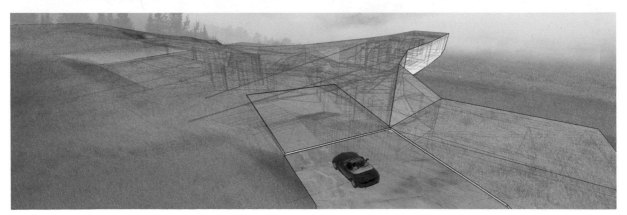

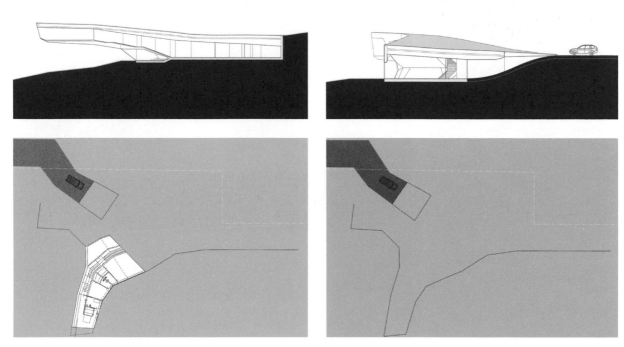

The sleeping quarters are laid out in a sequence along a 25 m (82 ft) cantilevered platform.

Aquarius

## Eduardo Souto de Moura

© Souto Moura Arquitectos

## Maia House
Maia, Portugal / 2007 / Photos: © Luís Ferreira Alves

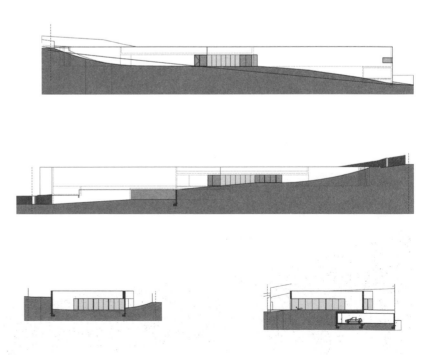

The perimeter walls of this residential development form an almost completely continuous box, except for the opening that serves as the entrance. The volume emerges subtly from the gentle incline of the site and is integrated into the landscape with extreme discretion.

**Souto Moura Arquitectos**
**Rua do Aleixo, 53, 1º A**
**4150-043 Porto, Portugal**
**Tel.: +351 226 187 547**

Eduardo Souto de Moura, born in Porto in 1952, is one of the leading lights in Portuguese architecture. A disciple of Álvaro Siza and Fernando Távora, he graduated from the University of Porto's School of Fine Arts and has taught at universities such as Harvard, Dublin and Lausanne. His works create a perfect blend of structure and context, and his residential projects, with their characteristic horizontal layout, are particularly well-known. Worthy of mention among the acknowledgments he has received are the 2005 FAD Award, the 2001 Heinrich Tessenow Medal, and the 2004 Secil Award.

The main level comprises two wings, one with common areas and the other with the sleeping quarters, both overlooking a green space.

Terraced on a hillside, this project includes both single-level and three-story residences. Each house is accessed through a small patio located next to the garage. Steel doors and panels line the main façades and give the complex a modern and discreet aspect.

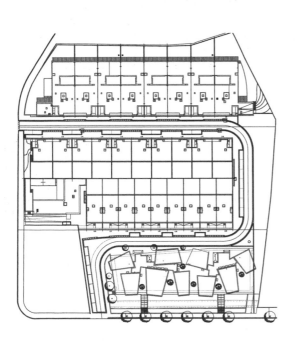

The interior layout of the homes follows an atypical pattern. For example, the living areas of the single-story houses are located at the rear.

This complex is located on the same plot as the Quinta da Avenida townhouses, which comprise the residential component of the development. A series of trapezoidal volumes are arranged over the site to house commercial activities and offices. All except for two only have one level.

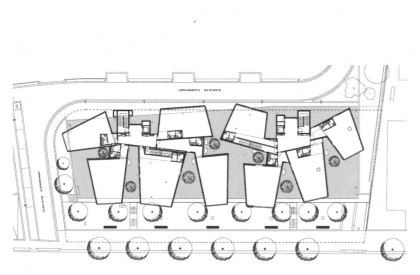

The main entrances open to the south. The floor-to-ceiling windows with barely a few inches of frame are a striking feature of the façades.

Located on one of Porto's main thoroughfares, Burgo Tower is raised over a platform that hides a two-level parking garage in its interior. The vertical nature of this project is unusual in Souto de Moura's work, although the architect gave the façade the elegance and slenderness typical of his style.

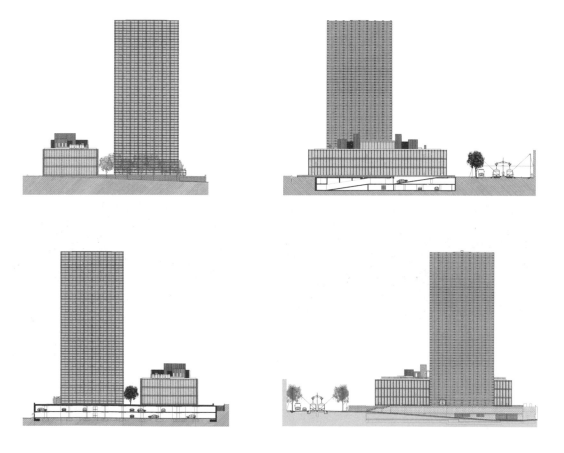

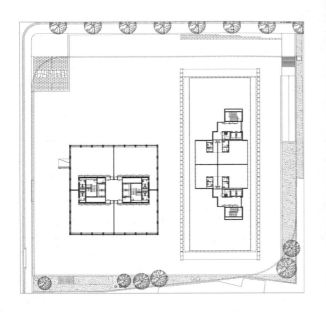

The contrast between the light-colored paving of the open area and the dark metal façade of the structures is one of the highlights of the project.

## Center for Contemporary Art
Bragança, Portugal / 2003 / Photos: © Luís Ferreira Alves

This reconversion project for an 18th century building also included the construction of a new structure, a large windowless box that would house the main part of the museum. Both structures are connected by a walkway and open out to a number of simple and elegant landscaped areas.

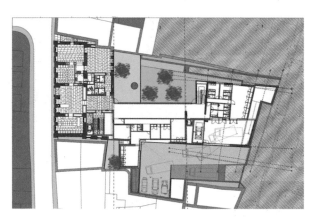

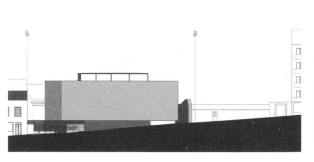

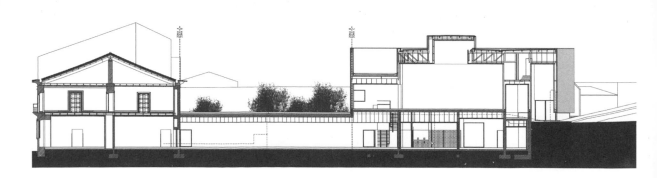

The transition from the old building to the newer parts occurs very naturally, with the white walls unifying the different styles.

Hydrus

## Senan Abdelqader

Mashrabiya
Jerusalem, Israel / 2007 / Renderings: © Senan Abdelqader Architects

This residence is located in the Palestinian town of Beit Safafa, between Jerusalem and Bethlehem. The reinterpretation of elements of traditional Arab architecture is clearly seen in the design, such as the pattern of geometric voids on the façade.

**Senan Abdelqader Architects**
Tel.: +972 26 76 00 82
www.senan-architects.com

Raised in Tayibe, an Arab village in northern Israel, Senan Abdelqader studied architecture in Germany. Returning to Israel, he taught at the Bezalel Academy of Art and Design. His studio is located in East Jerusalem and is responsible for important projects such as the Um El-Fahem Museum, and has participated in major exhibitions like the São Paulo Architecture Biennale.

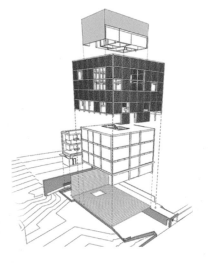

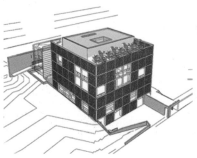

The structural concrete grid leaves some squares without cladding in order to connect the garden with the interior.

From the outside, this house rises like a composition of hanging or floating volumes that are relatively independent of each other while linked on the different levels.

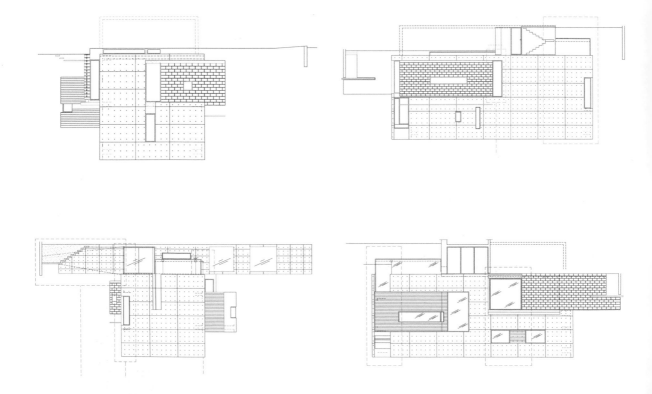

The apparently random combination of rectangular spaces brings interesting visual impact to the design.

The scarcity of resources in Palestine was largely behind the features of this project. This striking structure is suspended over the site like a bridge and lookout, perhaps a metaphor alluding to the struggle and resistance of the Palestinian people.

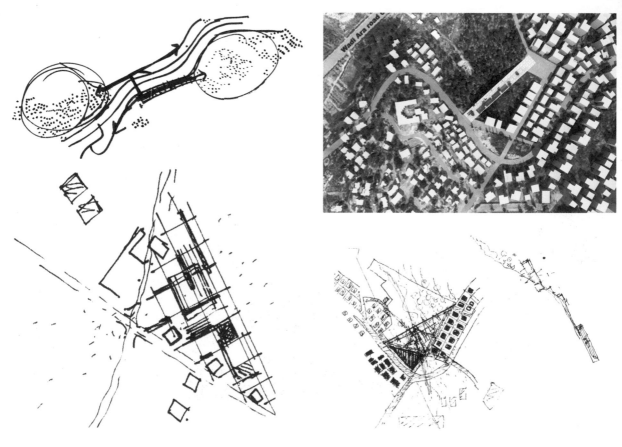

The upper level is designed as a large open-air gallery, with green spaces and exhibition areas.

Grus

## Kimmo Lintula, Niko Sirola & Mikko Summanen

© Marko Huttunen

K2S
Olympiastadion Eteläkaarre C1
0025 Helsinki, Finland
Tel.: +35 89 6831 3961
www.k2s.fi

Born between 1970 and 1971, the three founding members of K2S studied at the Helsinki University of Technology, where they currently teach. Since 2003 the studio has won important architectural competitions in Finland, among them the project to build a new canopy for the Olympic stadium in Helsinki. Among the awards received by the firm are the Architectural Review Emerging Architecture Award and the Chicago Athenaeum International Architecture Award.

## Enter
Sipoo, Finland / 2007 / Photos: © Marko Huttunen

This new L-shaped college building occupies the last lot in a corner of the school campus. The curved glass façades not only open up the school to the community, but also enable visual contact to be made between classrooms.

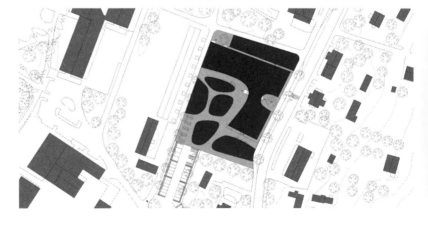

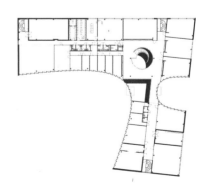

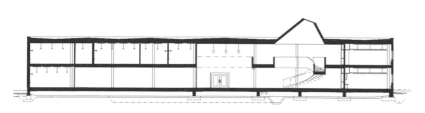

The concrete stairway, cast on-site, marks the center of the main foyer.

The winning project for this hospital in the Finnish town of Espoo was christened "orchid" by the architects, and the floor plan in fact traces a flower-like silhouette. The design includes a series of free-form units with rooms arranged around courtyards.

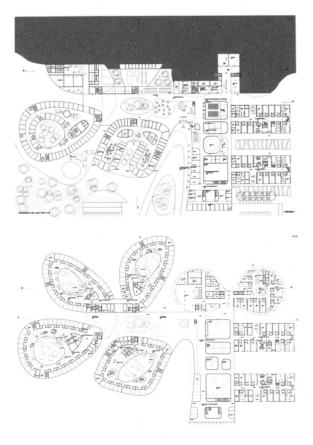

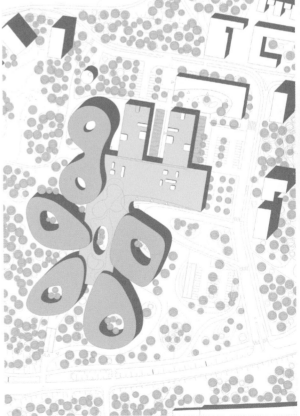

Green areas divide the different buildings and create transit areas.

## Olympic Stadium
Helsinki, Finland / 2005 / Photos: © Marko Huttunen

With a cost of 8,6 million dollars (6 million euros), the new cantilevered canopy of the Helsinki Olympic stadium protects a large area of bleachers and provides a strong element of drama to the view of the venue.

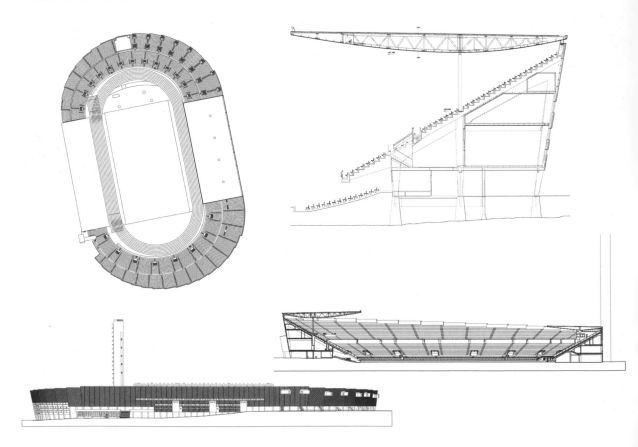

The elegant wooden cladding of the underside is particularly unique in this type of sports venue.

## Wooden Chapel

**Helsinki, Finland / To be determined / Renderings: © K2S**

This small wooden chapel resembles a beehive and offers a place for quiet meditation in one of Helsinki's busiest commercial precincts, in the middle of a square that enhances the sculptural nature of the building.

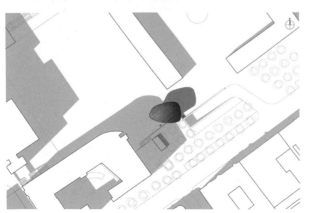

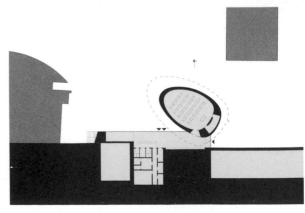

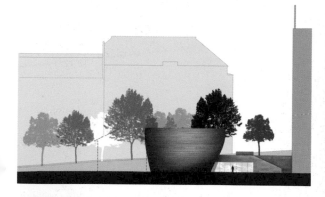
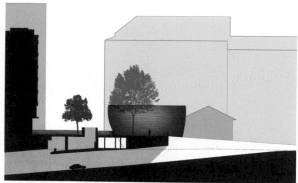

In the interior, indirect top-lighting creates a relaxed atmosphere and softens the honey color of the walls.

This summer residence, built by the owner of a drugstore, is located on the shore of a lake in southeast Finland. Aside from the main building, there are a number of wooden structures that serve as guesthouses, and two saunas.

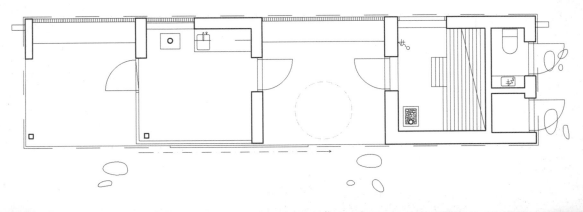

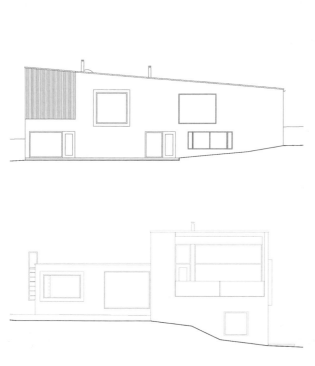

The interiors make ample use of wood, matching the style of the house with the pine woods outside.

Horologium

## Andreas Schmitzer

© Project A01 Architects

Project A01 Architects
Mariahilfer Strasse 101-2-27
1060 Vienna, Austria
Tel.: +43 1 526 88 26
www.schmitzer.com

Andreas Schmitzer was born in Salzburg in 1966 and studied in Vienna, Salzburg and Michigan. Between 1994 and 2005 he was an assistant professor in the Spatial Design Department of the Vienna University of Technology. In 2005 he established Project A01 Architects, projects from which have won competitions such as their design for the interiors of Austrian Airlines lounges.

## Aparthotel Zenta

Split, Croatia / To be determined / Renderings: © Project A01 Architects

© Project A01 Architects

This apartment building is only 500 m (1,640 ft) from the historic center of Split. With two basement levels, three above-ground levels and a penthouse, the shape of the building makes the greatest use of the size of the site.

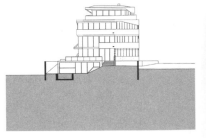

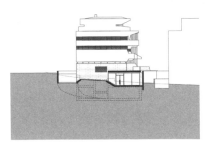

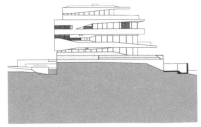

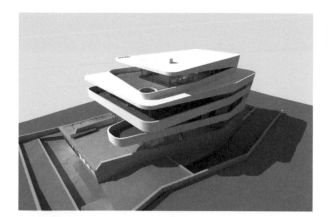

The series of terraces and balconies take advantage of privileged sea views.

This building is a modern entertainment center with a restaurant and bar, in addition to a space for boat exhibitions. It is clearly the architect's intention to simulate the sinuous forms of recreational craft, and to have as many windows as possible face the water.

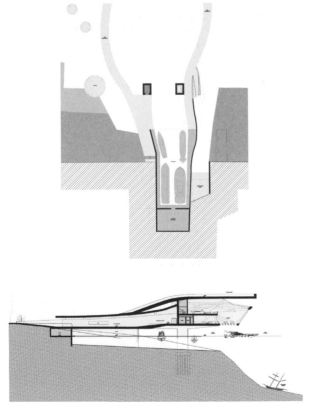

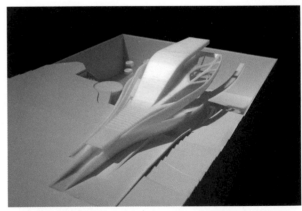

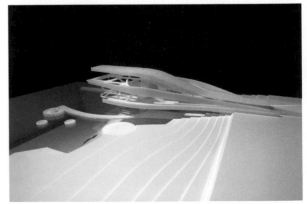

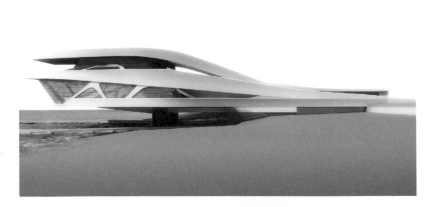

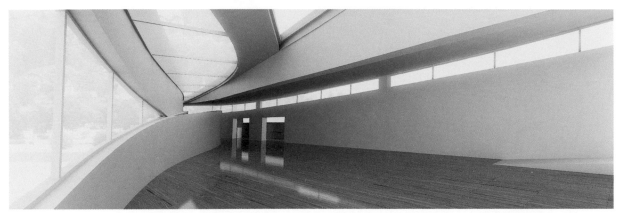

Transit areas are laid out in the same way as the deck of a boat, accentuating the source of inspiration for the project.

For the design of this luxury home, the concept behind the interiors was almost as important as that of the landscaped areas, which actually penetrate the interior space to a large degree. The lower level contains guest rooms while the upper level opens up to the sky and extends to a broad terrace.

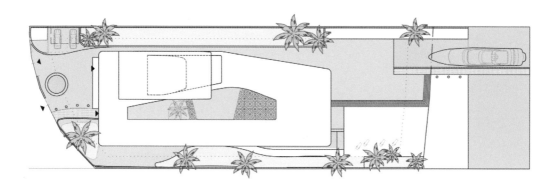

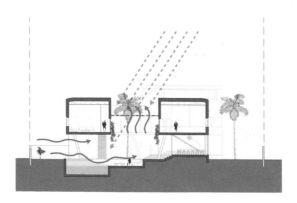

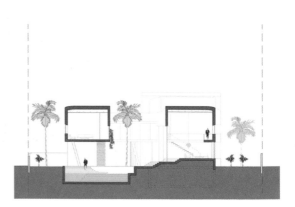

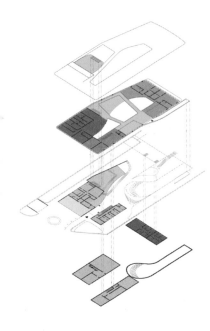

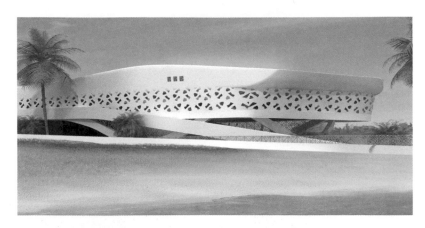

Three open courtyards provide natural ventilation, and the sea views are present in practically all parts of the house.

The base of this residence runs parallel to the incline of the terrain and is divided into different areas. The series of patios and terraces flow seamlessly into the interior spaces to create the illusion of a single unit.

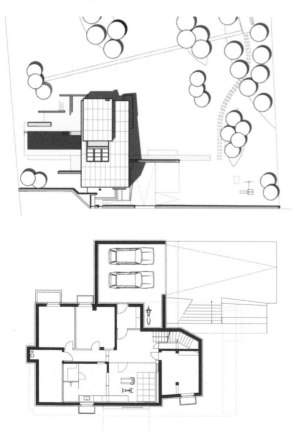

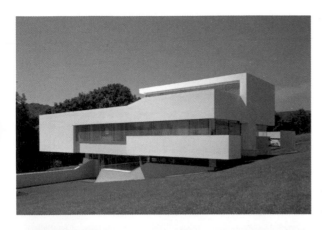

The interior steel columns are as narrow as possible so as not to obstruct the flow.

Fornax

## Giorgio Bottega
## & Henning Ehrhardt

© Bottega & Ehrhardt Architekten

**Bottega & Ehrhardt Architekten**
**Senefelderstrasse, 77 A**
**70176 Stuttgart, Germany**
**Tel.: +49 71 163 30 33 30**
**www.be-arch.com**

Giorgio Bottega was born in Rosenfeld, Germany, in 1967. He studied at the Stuttgart University of Applied Sciences and the Barcelona School of Architecture in the years from 1989 through 1995. He worked in several architectural firms between 1987 and 1997. Henning Ehrhardt was born in 1966 and studied architecture in Stuttgart and Zurich from 1986 through 1991. Both architects founded a studio together in 1998. Among their most outstanding projects are House B and House S, for which they were nominated for the Mies van der Rohe Award in 2003.

## House M
Stuttgart, Germany / 2004 / Photos: © David Franck

The remodeling of this house left few traces of the original appearance of the building. Reorganized on two levels, the roof was rebuilt as a rectangular steel box.

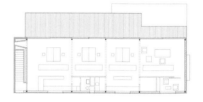

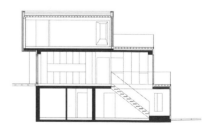

New expanses of glass connect the interior with a large terrace.

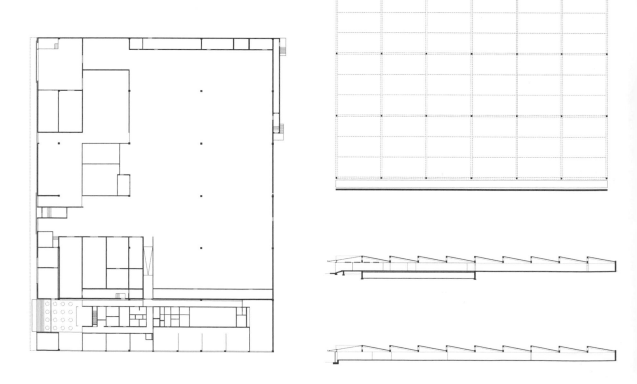

JOHANN MAIER GMBH

Remodeling of the Johann Maier factory meant a complete renovation for the company. The new offices feature elegant horizontal lines and the brilliant finish of the materials.

The remodeling left large modern open-plan interior spaces that are both discreet and elegant.

Designed to form part of the much talked about hundred villas development in Ordos, China, the residence for Lot 42 is a very compact black cube with a series of protruding volumes, cantilevered out in different directions.

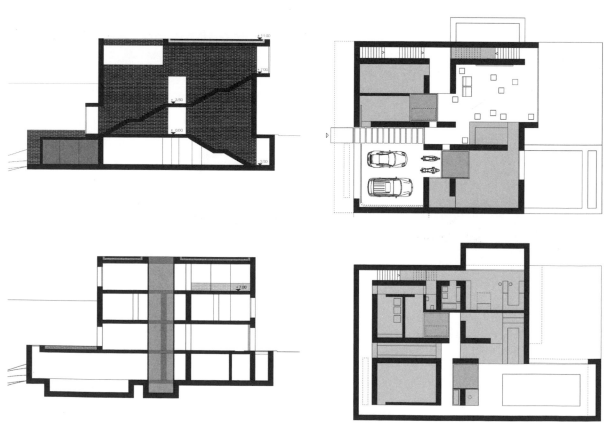

The building has a reinforced concrete skeleton perforated with black aluminum frames to hold windows.